BEYOND
ALL RELIGION

BY SAMUEL BUTLER

Beyond Mythical and Outrageously FORGED Religious Origins, and SCRIPTURES and Practices that Support Intolerance, Violence and Even War

A Peaceful World

Awaits

Published by Ø Shinelight Publications, 12355 SW 129 COURT, SUITE 10-197, MIAMI, FLORIDA , 33186-6406

Cover designs by **Ing. Fabián Gutiérrez**

Front Cover: Beyond the symbols of the four main religions- Christianity with the cross, Islam with the star and crescent, Judaism with the six pointed Star of David, and the symbol of Mormonism (the angel Moroni blowing the trumpet) are transformational rays filtering through the prism to a humanistic future of peace, tranquility, and spirituality.

ISBN-10:098523590X
ISBN-13:978-0-9852359-0-1
Library of Congress Control Number: 2011906005
Religion / Spirituality
The Code for Global Ethics

Eusebius "the first thoroughly dishonest historian of antiquity" and Emperor Constantine invent Christianity.
Violence, intolerance, and hate in all major religions
Mythical and forged origins of religion
Religious fraud

The Ten Principles For a Global Rational Humanism

Published by Ø Shinelight Publications,
12355 SW 129 COURT
SUITE 10-197
MIAMI, FLORIDA
 33186

BEYOND ALL RELIGION

SOME QUOTES ABOUT RELIGION
"When one person suffers from a delusion, it is called insanity. When many people suffer from a delusion it is called religion." - **Robert M. Pirsig, Zen and the Art of Motorcycle Maintenance**

"Faith is believing what you believe ain't so." **– Mark Twain**
"Faith doesn't give you the answers. It just stops you asking the questions." **– Frater Ravus**

"Religion is regarded by the common people as true, by the wise as false, and by the rulers as useful." **– Seneca the Younger (4 BCE-65 CE)**

"It is a truism that almost any sect, cult, or religion will legislate its creed into law if it acquires the political power to so." - **Sir Arthur C. Clark**

"Religion is comparable to a childhood neurosis." **– Sigmund Freud**

"Guilt: Punishing yourself before God doesn't." **– Alan Cohen**
"With or without religion, you would have good people doing good things and evil people doing evil things. But for good people to do evil things, that takes religion." **– Steven Weinberg**

"Anyone who engages in the practice of psychotherapy confronts every day the devastation wrought by the teachings of religion." – **Dr. Nathanial Branden, psychologist and author.**

"What have been Christianity's fruits? More or less in all places, pride and indolence in the Clergy, ignorance and servility in the laity; in both, superstition, bigotry and persecution." – **James Madison, 4th U.S. President**

"A man's ethical behavior should be based effectually on sympathy, education, and social ties; no religious basis is necessary. Man would indeed be in a poor way if he had to be restrained by fear of punishment and hope of reward after death. " – **Albert Einstein**

"You can't convince a believer of anything; for their belief is not based on evidence. It's based upon a deep-seated need to believe." - **Carl Sagan**

ACKNOWLEDGMENTS:
For editing help, Rosemary Zitek, Jorge Desanti, Geoffrey West, Paula Friedman, Ing. Fabián Gutiérrez, and especially my wife, Karen, of whom I say "She is the stuff that DREAMS are made of." For book structural guidance, Julio Bustos and Gilda Aburto, and for research and pagination, Vicky Kieke."

TABLE OF CONTENTS

FORWARD

Samuel can recall the time he became a skeptical free thinker. It was at Berkeley in Professor's Telfer Speech class. (It was much more than about speechmaking. It was about questioning your own and other's beliefs. It was about thinking critically-being skeptical, if you will).

As time went by Samuel became increasingly critical of the role organized religion plays in our lives. Blind unquestioning obedience to tradition, scripture and leadership has only led to separation and divisiveness, fostering hatred and intolerance for other people's religions. The idea of a benevolent cooperating community is the least concern of most of today's religions.

The issue of religion sponsored violence led Samuel to write his first book "A Pox on All Their Houses." A book dealing on how established religions actually encourage, in SCRIPTURE and their practices, support and sanction violence against other religions in a destructive effort of dominance and exploitation. As Christopher Hitchens once said "religion poisons everything." The proof of this statement is in the long history of wars and persecutions engendered by all religions such as the Crusades, the Inquisition, the Thirty Year War, and the current conflict between the Shiites and the Sunnis.

Religion's insidious control of people's personal lives often destroy family relationships. It commands who you should marry in spite of your true love. All these in the name of religion and its God.

You need an open mind to read this book. You would have to leave your baggage at the door. In return you will learn how to be a better person and someone with an open heart.

Jorge Luis Desanti, Professional Language Interpreter (including live emergency 911 U.S. calls and live on the phone for courts and police).

Bachelor of Science in Accounting. Accounting for HBO and various movie production companies.

INTRODUCTION

You may feel very uncomfortable with the information this book presents. All I ask is that you keep an open mind as a seeker of truth and open to a change to some of your beliefs if you feel it is proper for you to do so.

This book is about the consequences of religion more than whether Christ rose from the dead (Krishna, Mithras, Osiris, Attis of Phrygia, Dionysus, all of whom besides being born on December 25th from a virgin mother, died and were resurrected, except for Mithras - who ascended directly without dying!) or whether the text of the verses of the Qur'an correspond exactly to those revealed to Muhammad directly as the words of God, delivered to Muhammad through the angel Gabriel.. It is more focused on how religious scriptures and writings have been misused to harm, torture or kill others who don't believe, or used for justification to do what most rational persons would consider evil.

Christopher Hitchens puts it not so "mildly" as he claims he does when he says "Religion poisons everything", and "Religion Kills" [2]. Included are some religious cover-ups such as the invention of Christianity, based upon numerous previous myths and outrageous forgeries accomplished around and after 325 A.D. for political purposes ordered by Emperor Constantine and accomplished by his friend Eusebius (Bishop of Caesarea in Palestine) who has been described as "the first thoroughly dishonest historian of antiquity". Destruction of previous conflicting documents and edifices followed, including the destruction of the Great Library of Alexandria.

This book is an attempt to create awareness of the true origins and the fraudulent and forged self-serving writings of the main religions. Their purpose is to control and mislead us to follow them, without question, essentially putting us in a prison in our

3

own minds. Like the elephant with the rope around one foot, it is easy for us to break free, but we don't know it. This book is an attempt to encourage us to follow an alternative, a humanitarian secular ethical road moving beyond all religion.

BEYOND ALL RELIGION

"Religion is something we can perhaps do without." - **Dalai Lama** From his book Ethics for the New Millennium.

He also said: "This is my simple religion. There is no need for temples; no need for complicated philosophy. Our own brain, our own heart is our temple; the philosophy is kindness." **Dalai Lama**

"More violence has occurred in the name of religion than for any other reason." **Deepak Chopra** in New York Times Bestseller "The Book of Secrets"

"I do not believe in the creed professed by the Jewish Church, by the Roman Church, by the Greek Church, by the Turkish Church, by the Protestant Church, nor by any Church that I know of. My own mind is my own Church." [Thomas Paine, The Age of Reason] (Influential founder of the United States)

THE INVENTION OF CHRISTIANITY

BEYOND CHRISTIANITY

"I like your Christ, I do not like your Christians, they are not Christlike." **Mahatma Gandhi**

Emperor Constantine

Christianity is a copycat religion created by Emperor Constantine (for political purposes) based upon a myth (The Persian savior god Mithra, crucified 600 B.C.? 400 B.C.?), which was based on other similar myths, all the way back to Krishna of India (a mythical god that some claim was "crucified" around 1200 B.C.). There were 16 mythical crucifixions before Christ.

The belief in the crucifixion of Gods was prevalent in various oriental or heathen countries long prior to the reported crucifixion of Christ. Of the 16 crucifixions, **most were born of a virgin and about half of them on December 25th.**

There were too many religions in Rome in 325 A.D. A Council was called in an endeavor to amalgamate the many religions of the Roman Empire into one. Christianity plagiarized older myths and legends historicized to suit the Roman Catholic Church while combining the numerous religions existing at the time (Krishna, Horus, Mithraism, Osirian, Isis, and many other mystery religions). For unity and to stop all the conflicts between the numerous religions...

CHRISTIANITY WAS INVENTED

Eusebius (Bishop of Caesarea in Palestine "Father of Church History") attended the Council of Nicaea in 325 A.D. and was a friend of Emperor Constantine. Eusebius "occupied the first seat on the right of the emperor and delivered the inaugural address on the emperor's behalf" Constantine instructed Eusebius to organize the compilation of a uniform collection of new writings developed from primary aspects of the religious texts submitted at the council. Eusebius has been described as follows: Jacob Burckhardt (19th century cultural historian) dismissed Eusebius as **"the first thoroughly dishonest historian of antiquity"**. He has been also described as "a political theologian". He favored doctoring his history in his own words to "be useful first to ourselves and afterwards to posterity". Edward Gibbon (18th century historian –"The Decline and Fall of the Roman Empire") dismissed his testimony on the number of martyrs and impugned his honesty.

(To be clear on this matter, I say don't trust Eusebius's reports of the Apostles or how the Apostles died, and be suspicious of all of his writings.) - **Author** Samuel Butler

From: "THE FORGED ORIGINS OF THE NEW TESTAMENT" by Tony Bushby
"Constantine was the ruling spirit at Nicaea and he ultimately decided upon a new god for them. To involve British factions, he ruled that the name of the great Druid god, *Hesus*, be

joined with the Eastern Savior-god, Krishna (*Krishna* is Sanskrit for *Christ*), and thus *Hesus Krishna* would be the official name of the new Roman god."

"Eusebius then arranged for scribes to produce fifty sumptuous copies to be written on parchment in a legible manner, and in a convenient portable form, by professional scribes thoroughly accomplished in their art (ibid.)."

BISHOP EUSEBIUS

"These orders, said Eusebius, were followed by the immediate execution of the work itself we sent him [Constantine] magnificently and elaborately bound volumes of three-fold and four-fold forms (Life of Constantine, vol. iv, p.36). They were the New Testimonies, and this is the first mention (c. 331) of the New Testament in the historical record. With his instructions fulfilled, Constantine then decreed that the New Testimonies would thereafter be called the word of the Roman Savior God (Life of Constantine, vol. iii, p. 29) and official to all presbyters sermonizing in the Roman Empire."

"He then ordered earlier presbyterial manuscripts and the records of the council burnt and declared that any man found concealing writings should be stricken off from his shoulders **(beheaded)**."

"None of these 50 new testaments exist today or are admitted to existing!

This new testament was the official book of the new unified religion of Constantine not the bible!

All other books to be burned ,that would include the Torah/old testament

It included burning the great library of Alexandria in Egypt 391 a.d."

The following is from:
http://en.wikipedia.org/wiki/Library_of_Alexandria

Socrates of Constantinople provides the following account of the destruction of the temples in Alexandria, in the fifth book of his *Historia Ecclesiastica*, written around 440:

"At the solicitation of Theophilus, Bishop of Alexandria, the emperor issued an order at this time for the demolition of the heathen temples in that city; commanding also that it should be put in execution under the direction of Theophilus. Seizing this opportunity, Theophilus exerted himself to the utmost to expose the pagan mysteries to contempt. And to begin with, he caused the Mithreum to be cleaned out, and exhibited to public view the tokens of its bloody mysteries. Then he destroyed the Serapeum, and the bloody rites of the Mithreum he publicly caricatured; the Serapeum also he showed full of extravagant superstitions, and he had the phalli of Priapus carried through the midst of the forum. ... Thus this disturbance having been terminated, the governor of Alexandria, and the commander-in-chief of the troops in Egypt, assisted Theophilus in demolishing the heathen temples."

Note from author: The "heathen" or "pagan" temples included the Serapeum.

THE SERAPEUM HOUSED THE GREAT LIBRARY OF ALEXANDRIA

Why there are no records of Jesus Christ?

Federic William Farrar

It is not possible to find in any legitimate religious or historical writings compiled between the beginning of the first century and well into the fourth century any reference to Jesus Christ and the spectacular events that the Church says accompanied his life.

This confirmation comes from Frederic Farrar (1831-1903) of Trinity College, Cambridge:
"It is amazing that history has not embalmed for us even one certain or definite saying or circumstance in the life of the Saviour of mankind ... there is no statement in all history that says anyone saw Jesus or talked with him. Nothing in history is more astonishing than the silence of contemporary writers about events relayed in the four Gospels." (The Life of Christ, Frederic W. Farrar, Cassell, London, 1874)

This situation arises from a conflict between history and New Testament narratives. Dr Tischendorf made this comment:

"We must frankly admit that we have no source of information with respect to the life of Jesus Christ other than ecclesiastic writings assembled during the fourth century." (Codex Sinaiticus, Dr Constantin von Tischendorf, British Library, London)

There is an explanation for those hundreds of years of silence: the construct of Christianity did not begin until after the first quarter of the fourth century, and that is why Pope Leo X (d.

1521) called Christ a "fable" (Cardinal Bembo: His Letters…, op. cit.), and later Pope Paul III expressed similar sentiments, saying that there was no valid document to demonstrate the existence of Christ. He confessed that "Jesus never existed", adding that he was "no other than the sun, adored in its Mithraic sect…"

BUT WAIT, WHAT DOES THE CATHOLIC CHURCH SAY ABOUT THIS?

You will be surprised:
From:
http://www.bibliotecapleyades.net/biblianazar/esp_biblianazar_40.htm

"What the Church doesn't want you to know.

It has often been emphasized that *Christianity* is unlike any other religion, for it stands or falls by certain events which are alleged to have occurred during a short period of time some 20 centuries ago. Those stories are presented in the New Testament, and as new evidence is revealed it will become clear that they do not represent historical realities."

The Church agrees, saying:
> "Our documentary sources of knowledge about the origins of Christianity and its earliest development are chiefly the New Testament Scriptures, the authenticity of which we must, to a great extent, take for granted." **(Catholic Encyclopedia, Farley ed., vol. iii, p. 712)**

The Church makes extraordinary admissions about its New Testament. For example, when discussing the origin of those writings,

> "the most distinguished body of academic opinion ever assembled" (Catholic Encyclopedias, Preface) admits that the Gospels "do not go back to the first century of the Christian era"
> **(Catholic Encyclopedia, Farley ed., vol. vi, p. 137, pp. 655-6).**

"This statement conflicts with priesthood assertions that the earliest Gospels were progressively written during the decades following the death of the Gospel *Jesus Christ*."

In a remarkable aside, the Church further admits that,
> "the earliest of the extant manuscripts [of the New Testament], it is true, do not date back beyond the middle of the fourth century AD"
> **(Catholic Encyclopedia, op. cit., pp. 656-7).**

"That is some 350 years after the time the Church claims that a *Jesus Christ* walked the sands of Palestine, and here the true story of Christian origins slips into <u>one of the biggest black holes in history</u>. There is, however, a reason why there were no New Testaments until the fourth century: they were not written until then, and here we find evidence of the greatest misrepresentation of all time.

It was British-born <u>Flavius Constantinus</u> (**Constantine**, originally *Custennyn* or *Custennin*) (272-337) who authorized the compilation of the writings now called the *New Testament*. "

Yes, but what about references to the four Gospels supposedly before the 3rd Century A.D.?

For example: What about Tacitus, Roman Historian, who wrote about the persecutions of the early "Christians"?

Regarding Tacitus, (Senator and Historian of the Roman Empire) these writings supporting the persecution were mysteriously found in the 15th century in the forests of Germany, following a reward offered by Leo X for old writings, and following a history of forgeries in Catholicism: In any case, there has been serious questions about the integrity of the famous passage about Christians.

From: http://www.earlychristianwritings.com/tacitus.html

Gordon Stein denied the authenticity of this passage, arguing:

(1) no corroborating evidence that Nero persecuted the Christians
(2) there was not a multitude of Christians in Rome at that date
(3) "Christian" was not a common term in the first century
(4) Nero was indifferent to various religions in his city
(5) Nero did not start the fire in Rome
(6) Tacitus does not use the name Jesus
(7) Tacitus assumes his readers know Pontius Pilate

YES, BUT WHAT ABOUT JOSEPHUS?

His reference to Jesus in Testimonium Flavianum has been claimed as a later addition, (**Forgery**-Author) not questioning the authenticity of the main work.

See:
http://www.truthbeknown.com/josephus.htm

13

YES, BUT WHAT ABOUT PLINY THE YOUNGER'S LETTER TO EMPEROR TRAJAN 112 A.D.?

(Pliny was not a contemporary of Jesus, and he never mentions "Jesus") Pliny the Younger (c. 61 – c. 112), the provincial governor of Pontus and Bithynia, wrote to Emperor Trajan c. 112 concerning how to deal with Christians, who refused to worship the emperor, and instead worshiped "Christus".

What about that?
Charles Guignebert, who does not doubt that Jesus of the Gospels lived in Gallilee in the 1st century, nevertheless dismisses this letter as acceptable historical evidence:
"Only the most robust credulity could reckon this assertion as admissible evidence for the historicity of Jesus" –

Charles Guignebert

http://en.wikipedia.org/wiki/Historicity_of_Jesus

Nevertheless, I was concerned about the possibility of far older Gospels when I was stating that Christianity was invented around 325 A.D., but the research thread leads back to Eusebius, the FORGER, ("Papias, quoted by Eusebius…").

Eusebius was the dishonest Church Father historian of antiquity who made up a lot of Church history. "we shall introduce into this history in general only those events which may be useful first to ourselves and afterwards to posterity". The research thread (about older Gospels) also leads to the "spurious" writings of Irenaeus:

http://www.sodahead.com/united-states/gospels-late-forgeries/blog-249881/

In any case, the Catholic Encyclopedia itself supports the thesis that the Gospels of Christianity were written no earlier than the 4th Century: "the earliest of the extant manuscripts [of the New Testament], it is true, do not date back beyond the middle of the fourth century AD"– (Catholic Encyclopedia, op. cit., pp. 656-7)

Pre-nicene so-called "Early Christian" (Gnostic?) writings, disagreed with each other, were riddled with conflict and forgeries, and were of questionable and confusing timing and origin , they were not coherent enough for an organized religion. This is well explained in the book "Lost Christianities The Battles for Scriptures and Faiths We Never Knew", by Bart D. Ehrman. So the myth of Mithra, the Persian Savior God, was chosen by Emperor Constantine and Bishop Eusebius ("the first thoroughly dishonest historian of antiquity") as the model to create the new religion , Christianity."

THE FOUNDING FATHERS WERE NOT CHRISTIANS

"The fable of Christ and his twelve apostles...is a parody of the sun and the twelve signs of the Zodiac, copied from the ancient religions of the Eastern world.... Everything told of Christ has reference to the sun. His reported resurrection is at sunrise, and that on the first day of the week; that is, on the day anciently dedicated to the sun, and from thence called Sunday..."
Thomas Paine, The Complete Religious and Theological Works of Thomas Paine (382)

"...the day will come when the mystical generation of Jesus, by the supreme being as his father in the womb of a virgin will be classed with the fable of the generation of Minerva in the brain of Jupiter."
Thomas Jefferson, The Adams-Jefferson Letters (594)

More from Thomas Paine:
"I do not believe in the creed professed by the Jewish church, by the Roman church, by the Greek church, by the Turkish church, by the Protestant church, nor by any church that I know of...Each of those churches accuse the other of unbelief; and for my own part, I disbelieve them all."

John Adams:
Late in life he wrote: "Twenty times in the course of my late reading, have I been upon the point of breaking out, "This would be the best of all possible worlds, if there were no religion in it!"

James Madison, fourth president and father of the Constitution, was not religious in any conventional sense. "Religious bondage shackles and debilitates the mind and unfits it for every noble enterprise."

Benjamin Franklin:
"As to Jesus of Nazareth…. I have, with most of the present dissenters in England, some doubts as to his Divinity."

Five founders who were skeptical of organized Christianity and couldn't be elected today Washington, Adams, Jefferson, Madison and Paine wouldn't pass the modern-day religious test for high office, argues policy analyst ROB BOSTON
Sunday, January 22, 2012

To hear the religious right tell it, men like George Washington, John Adams, Thomas Jefferson and James Madison were 18th-century versions of Jerry Falwell in powdered wigs and stockings. Nothing could be further from the truth.

Unlike many of today's candidates, the founders didn't find it necessary to constantly wear religion on their sleeves. They considered faith a private affair.

Contrast them to former Speaker of the House Newt Gingrich (who says he wouldn't vote for an atheist for president because nonbelievers lack the proper moral grounding to guide the American ship of state), Texas Gov. Rick Perry (who hosted a prayer rally and issued an infamous ad accusing President Barack Obama of waging a "war on religion") and former Pennsylvania Sen. Rick Santorum (whose uber-Catholicism leads him to oppose not just abortion but birth control).

There was a time when Americans voted for candidates who were skeptical of core concepts of Christianity like the Trinity, the divinity of Jesus and the virgin birth. The question is, could any of them get elected today? The sad answer is probably not.

Here are five founding fathers whose views on religion would most likely doom them to defeat today:

GEORGE WASHINGTON

The father of our country was nominally an Anglican but seemed more at home with Deism. The language of the Deists sounds odd to today's ears because it's a theological system of thought that has fallen out of favor. Deists believed in God but didn't necessarily see him as active in human affairs. He set things in motion and then stepped back.

Washington often employed Deistic terms. His god was a "supreme architect" of the universe. Washington saw religion as necessary for good moral behavior but didn't accept all Christian dogma. He seemed to have a special gripe against communion and would usually leave services before it was offered.

Washington was widely tolerant of other beliefs. He is the author of one of the great classics of religious liberty -- the letter to Touro Synagogue (1790) -- in which he assured America's Jews that they would enjoy complete religious liberty in America; not mere toleration in an officially "Christian" nation. He outlines a vision of a multi-faith society where all are free.

"All possess alike liberty of conscience and immunities of citizenship," Washington wrote. "It is now no more that toleration is spoken of, as if it was by the indulgence of one class of people that another enjoyed the exercise of their inherent natural rights. For happily the government of the United States, which gives to bigotry no sanction, to persecution no assistance, requires only that they who live under its protection should demean themselves as good citizens."

Stories of Washington's deep religiosity, such as tales of him praying in the snow at Valley Forge, are pious legends invented after his death.

JOHN ADAMS

The man who followed Washington as president was a Unitarian, although he was raised a Congregationalist and never officially left that church. Adams rejected belief in the Trinity and the divinity of Jesus, core concepts of Christian dogma. In his personal writings, Adams makes it clear that he considered some Christian dogma to be incomprehensible.

In February 1756, Adams wrote in his diary about a discussion he had had with a conservative Christian named Major Greene. The two argued over the divinity of Jesus and the Trinity. Questioned on the matter of Jesus' divinity, Greene fell back on an old standby: some matters of theology are too complex and mysterious for we puny humans to understand.

Adams was not impressed. In his diary he wrote, "Thus mystery is made a convenient cover for absurdity."

As president, Adams signed the famous Treaty of Tripoli, which boldly stated, "The government of the United States of America is not in any sense founded on the Christian Religion ..."

THOMAS JEFFERSON

It's almost impossible to define Jefferson's subtle religious views in a few words. As he once put it, "I am a sect by myself, as far as I know."

But one thing is clear: His skepticism of traditional Christianity is well established. Our third president did not believe in the Trinity, the virgin birth, the divinity of Jesus, the resurrection, original sin and other core Christian doctrines. He was hostile to many conservative Christian clerics, whom he believed had perverted the teachings of that faith.

Jefferson once famously observed to Adams, "And the day will come when the mystical generation of Jesus, by the supreme being as his father in the womb of a virgin, will be classed with the fable of the generation of Minerva in the brain of Jupiter."

Although not an orthodox Christian, Jefferson admired Jesus as a moral teacher. In one of his most unusual acts, Jefferson edited the New Testament, cutting away the stories of miracles and divinity and leaving behind a very human Jesus, whose teachings Jefferson found "sublime." This "Jefferson Bible" is a remarkable document -- and it would ensure his political defeat today. (Imagine the TV commercials the religious right would run: Thomas Jefferson hates Jesus! He mutilates Bibles!)

Jefferson was confident that a coolly rational form of religion would take root in the fertile intellectual soil of America. And he took political stands that would infuriate today's religious right. He refused to issue proclamations calling for days of prayer and fasting, saying that such religious duties were no part of the chief executive's job. His assertion that the First Amendment erects a "wall of separation between church and state" still rankles the religious right today.

JAMES MADISON
Jefferson's close ally would be similarly unelectable today. Madison is perhaps the most enigmatic of all the founders when it comes to religion. Scholars still debate his religious views.

Nominally Anglican, Madison, some of his biographers believe, was really a Deist. He went through a period of enthusiasm for Christianity as a young man, but this seems to have faded. Unlike many of today's politicians, who eagerly wear religion on their sleeves and brag about the ways their faith will guide their policy decisions, Madison was notoriously reluctant to talk publicly about his religious beliefs.

Madison was perhaps the strictest church-state separationist among the founders, taking stands that make the ACLU look like a bunch of pikers. He opposed government-paid chaplains in Congress and in the military. As president, Madison rejected a proposed census because it involved counting people by profession. For the government to count the clergy, Madison said, would violate the First Amendment.

Madison, who wrote the Constitution and the Bill of Rights, also opposed government prayer proclamations. He issued a few during the War of 1812 at the insistence of Congress but later concluded that his actions had been unconstitutional. He vetoed legislation granting federal land to a church and a plan to have a church in Washington care for the poor through a largely symbolic charter. In both cases, he cited the First Amendment.

THOMAS PAINE

Paine never held elective office, but as a pamphleteer his stirring words helped rally Americans to independence. Washington ordered that Paine's pamphlet "The American Crisis" be read aloud to the Continental Army as a morale booster on Dec. 23, 1776. "Common Sense" was similarly popular with the people. These seminal documents were crucial to winning over the public to the side of independence.

So Paine's a hero, right? He was also a radical Deist whose later work, "The Age of Reason," still infuriates fundamentalists.

In the tome, Paine attacked institutionalized religion and all of the major tenets of Christianity. He rejected prophecies and miracles and called on readers to embrace reason. The Bible, Paine asserted, can in no way be infallible. He called the god of the Old Testament "wicked" and the entire Bible "the pretended word of God." (There go the Red States!)

What can we learn from this? Americans have the right to reject candidates for any reason, including their religious beliefs. But they ought to think twice before tossing someone aside just because he or she is skeptical of orthodox Christianity. After all, that description includes some of our nation's greatest leaders.

Rob Boston, a native of Altoona and graduate of Indiana University of Pennsylvania, is a senior policy analyst at Americans United for Separation of Church and State. This originally appeared at Alternet.org.

http://tinyurl.com/85cd9e7

First published on January 22, 2012 Here:
http://www.post-gazette.com/pg/12022/1204849-109-0.stm#ixzz1lr2tgfBZ

THE UNITED STATES WAS NOT, IN ANY SENSE, FOUNDED ON THE CHRISTIAN RELIGION

It's in a treaty.

From: http://en.wikipedia.org/wiki/Treaty_of_Tripoli

..."receiving ratification unanimously from the U.S. Senate on June 7, 1797 and signed by Adams, taking effect as the law of the land on June 10, 1797.

The Treaty is much discussed in the 21st century because of the text of article 11, as ratified by the Senate:

As the Government of the United States of America is not, in any sense, founded on the Christian religion; as it has in itself no character of enmity against the laws, religion, or tranquility, of Mussulmen; and, as the said States never entered into any war, or act of hostility against any Mahometan nation, it is declared by the parties, that no pretext arising from religious opinions, shall ever produce an interruption of the harmony existing between the two countries."

THE TEN PRINCIPLES FOR A GLOBAL RATIONAL HUMANISM THE CODE FOR GLOBAL ETHICS

1. DIGNITY: Proclaim the natural dignity and inherent worth of all human beings.
2. RESPECT: Respect the life and property of others.
3. TOLERANCE: Be tolerant of others' beliefs and lifestyles.
4. SHARING: Share with those who are less fortunate and assist those who are in need of help.

5. NO DOMINATION: Do not dominate through lies or otherwise.

6. NO SUPERSTITION: Rely on reason, logic, and science to understand the Universe and to solve life's problems.

7. CONSERVATION: Conserve and improve the Earth's natural environment.

8. NO WAR: Resolve differences and conflicts without resorting to war or violence.

9. DEMOCRACY: Rely on political and economic democracy to organize human affairs.

10. EDUCATION: Develop one's intelligence and talents through education and effort.

From "The Code for Global Ethics, Ten Humanist Principles" by Rodrigue Tremblay, with Preface by Paul Kurtz. Published 2010 by Prometheus Books.

17 YEAR ADVISOR TO THE POPE EXPOSES BIBLE FRAUD AND FORGERY

Retired highly regarded priest, who for 17 years (1980-1997) served as an advisor to the Pope, exposes bible forgery and fraud.

 Dr. Miceal Ledwith achieved distinction as a catholic theologian who received international recognition for academic and professional accomplishment. An esteemed professor of Systemic Theology, president of the University of Maymooth , Ireland (National University of Ireland-Author) and fulfilling a seventeen year appointment as advisor to the Pope on the Holy See's international Theological Commission. Yet at the height of his career, he walked away to pursue a completely different kind of spiritual life – one of humble, internal initiation and transformation. He talks about an enormous upheaval after the Second Vatican Council:

"I think most of my contemporaries were doing the same thing that I was and pondering the same thoughts, maybe not as intensely, but they were certainly as aware of those theories as I was. There were many people in positions of authority in the church that were contemplating the inconsistencies, and a lot of them ran afoul of religious authority. This is of course something that had always occurred throughout the history of Christianity.

"I spoke with someone the other day that insisted on the importance of holding on to some permanently valid religious truth. I asked "And where might we hope to find that in the gospels of the New Testament, for example? Let me suggest something."

"Go to the Vatican Library today and look at the oldest manuscript that we have of the New Testament, which is known as the Codex Vaticanus', and was probably one of the bibles commissioned by Constantine. Another one to look at is in the British Library called codex Sinaiticus' which was discovered in Mount Sinai at St. Catherine's Monastery. Look at those two texts, both from the 4TH century, and try to find the famous story of Jesus rescuing the lady who is being stoned for adultery in John's Gospel Chapter 8. It is a very powerful story, but it is not contained in either of those manuscripts, which means that story was inserted into the text of the New Testament for the first time at least as late as the 4th century if not later. I can give you a hundred other examples."

(Above from Super Consciousness Magazine Fall 2010 page 64)

RELIGION POISONS POSSIBLE TRUE LOVES FROM MARRYING

Friday, January 20, 2012
4:25 AM

When I was an undergraduate student at University of California, Berkeley, I was seated on a long table in the University Library with students like myself on either side. I was a little tired in the library, and put my head down on my book to rest. When I raised my head up, an attractive dark-haired girl seated across from me was looking at me, smiling, asked "Do you study by osmosis?" (Some people say one can absorb a book by resting their heads

upon a book!).

Amused, I started a conversation with her. Her name was Barbara.

We spent a lot of time together. I had a car, and she lived in San Leandro, about 25 minutes south of Berkeley. One time we stayed up all night to see the sunrise. We never consummated our relationship, but came close. She had incredibly soft skin, especially in the neck and shoulder area. She was very intelligent, and we coincided in liberal thinking, in a time of social germinating upheaval. It was 1958. We attended a meeting against the hydrogen bomb, among others.

I eventually asked her to marry me.

First, she wanted to meet my family. Both of my parents had died, but I had brothers in Northern California. We went and visited (briefly) my brother Bob and his wife Mary in San Francisco, and my brother Tom and his wife Shirley in Santa Cruz, and my sister Kay, in Santa Clara County, as I recall.

I believe Barbara truly loved me, but there came an obstacle, other than her family being wealthier than my family. (Barbara's father owned a factory in San Leandro).

There was something else. She was Jewish.

My remaining family at the time were all Christians. As it turned out, her very rich grandfather did not want her to marry a gentile, and if she did, she was told that he would dis-inherit (disown?) her. She would be an outcast to an important part of her family.

I seemed to get along very well with Barbara's mother, and didn't see much of her father.

So because of religion, two people in love, couldn't marry.

The irony of the story is that I found out later that my grandparents on my father side are both buried in a Jewish Cemetery in New York. My mother was full blooded Norwegian. Her mother had been a lady in waiting to the Queen of Norway.

Her father was a Lutheran minister.

My mother, I heard, told my Jewish father that she would marry him only if he agreed to bring up the children as Christians.

My father agreed, and his Jewish background was suppressed.

My mother, Catherine Dahl Butler, eventually had 6 children, me being the last. I didn't know I was part Jewish until I was 18.

Later, doing genealogy, I found out that I am probably close **to 50% Jewish!**

Maybe her grandfather wouldn't have dis-inherited her if he was informed of that information.

The point of this story is that religion kills and/or poisons potential marriages between otherwise compatible loves.

I later married Marcy, the mother of my son Matthew. Marcy was brought up Catholic, but she was not devout. We needed a facility in which to get married, but we were forbidden to marry in the Catholic Church, because she had a previous divorce. We were married by a Justice of the Peace in San Francisco City Hall instead.

In a perfect world Beyond Religion, many potential marriages between very otherwise compatible potential partners wouldn't be arbitrarily blocked.

Does this odyssey matter to me, today? I am now happily married after several attempts at a lasting married relationship. Besides that, Barbara's family (grandfather?) probably would have tried to make me convert to Judaism, and I would be a captive IN religion, not FREE and BEYOND religion.

In many religions, to marry a person of a different religion means being ostracized from your church/temple and even family.

I could even mean death in parts of the Middle East.

THEY MURDERED THE POPE!

There is violence even within the Vatican Holy See.
By Samuel Butler 03/31/11

When I was a commercial real estate broker, I was involved in a large land transaction, later completed on a property in Marin County, California. My interested party in the purchase was Bruce Connor, associated with the Howard S. Wright Corporation of Seattle, a huge and important developer. They built the Space Needle in Seattle.

Bruce told me the following story. Bruce went to Rome with a friend, and while he was there, his friend went to the Vatican, where his friend had a personal friend in the Holy See, which acts and speaks for the whole Catholic Church.

http://en.wikipedia.org/wiki/Holy_See

When Connor's friend came back from the Holy See, he told my client Connor, "THEY MURDERED THE POPE!". Connor was told that there was no autopsy, no time of death, and a deep mystery.

His friend told Connor that the Pope couldn't handle the job, and there is only one way to go if you are Pope and can't handle the job. The Pope only served as Pope for 33 days. It was that simple. He couldn't handle the job, and he couldn't resign. At that time, 1978, the Pope was supposedly infallible on dogmatic statements. It would be strange to have an "infallible" Pope resign.

The Pope was John Paul I. He lasted only 33 days. He chose the first double name in the history of the papacy.

I later did research on this and found that this "humble" and "smiling" Pope , as he was known from Venice, far from being a pushover for the hierarchy of the Church, wanted to:

1. Fire the Cardinal of Chicago
2. Re-open birth control
3. Personally investigate the Vatican Bank

He was poisoned.

1. There was no time of death stated.
2. There was no autopsy.
3. There still is no death certificate to this day

There were 6 suspects to the murder.

One was Roberto Calvi, Chairman of the "Vatican Bank", and known as "God's Banker", and one was Paul Marcinkus http://en.wikipedia.org/wiki/Paul_Marcinkus, who was President of the " Vatican Bank" at the time of the Pope's mysterious death.

It turned up later that 1.3 billion dollars vanished in the later collapse of that bank. It ended up that five of the 6 suspects died under mysterious circumstances. For example, Roberto Calvi committed suicide in London, after missing from Milan, Italy for 9 days, by going to the Blackfriars Bridge in London, climbing to the underneath of it and putting a rope around his neck to hang himself!

The sole survivor of the six suspects after a period of time turned out to be coincidentally enough, the head of the Vatican Bank, Paul Marcinkus, who died in Sun City, Arizona on February 20, 2006.

There is a book about this, the murder of this Pope, John Paul I, I found in my research. It's called "In God's Name", by David Yallop, a world-wide best seller.

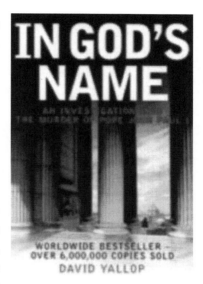

http://www.amazon.co.uk/Gods -Name-Investigation-into- Murder/dp/1845294963

Having written a book about all four of the main religions supporting Violence, Intolerance, and Even War, this article shows one of the religions had **MURDER** within its own structure, **AT THE TOP, including even within the last 33 years.**

There's more: Other Popes who have been murdered.

From **Wikipedia: List of 10 Popes who allegedly have been murdered. Five of them by poisoning.**
http://tinyurl.com/3mu33zd

Also, according to this, http://www.answering-islam.org/Silas/mo-death.htm, Muhammad also died of being poisoned (by a Jewish woman). Intrigue and politics and power plays are not so unusual in the Church. One time there were 3 popes! Yes, three at the same time (sometimes the "other Popes" were called "Anti-Popes".)

CHRISTIANITY

"I don't believe in the divinity of Christ, and there are many other postulates of the orthodox creed to which I cannot subscribe." - **William Howard Taft, 27th U.S. President**

"Historically, it is quite doubtful whether Christ ever existed at all, and if He did we do not know anything about Him." Bertrand Russell, "Why I am not a Christian."

David Jenkins, a former Anglican Bishop of Durham and university professor, has stated that "There is absolutely no certainty in the New Testament about anything of importance."

MATTHEW

* Jesus recommends that to avoid sin we cut off our hands and pluck out our eyes. This advice is given immediately after he says that anyone who looks with lust at any women commits adultery. 5:29-30

* Jesus says that most people will go to hell. 7:13-14

* Jesus sends some devils into a herd of pigs, causing them to run off a cliff and drown in the waters below. 8:32

* Jesus condemns entire cities to dreadful deaths and to the eternal torment of hell because they didn't care for his preaching. 11:20-24

LUKE

* Jesus says that entire cities will be violently destroyed and the inhabitants "thrust down to hell" for not "receiving" his disciples. 10:10-15

Christianity was based on previous myths:

WHO WAS THIS?

His birth in a grotto was attended by Magi who followed a star from the East. They brought "gifts of gold, frankincense and myrrh" and the newborn baby was adored by shepherds. ____, one of a trinity, stood on a rock, the emblem of the foundation of his religion, and was anointed with honey. After a last supper with Helios and 11 other companions, ____ was crucified on a cross, bound in linen, placed in a rock tomb and rose on the third day or around 25 March (the full moon at the spring equinox, a time now called Easter after the Babylonian goddess Ishtar). The fiery destruction of the universe was a major doctrine of _____ism-a time in which _____ promised to return in person to Earth and save deserving souls. Devotees of ____ partook in a sacred communion banquet of bread and wine.

Archeologists have found as many as 718 monuments or statues of ____ at Ostia (near Rome-Author) and close to 300 in Rome. A ____ shrine was uncovered under St. Paul's cathedral.____ was a god, a son of a god, born of a virgin on December 25.

WHO WAS THIS?

His name was Mithra, the messiah of the first kings of the Persian Empire around 400 B.C. (600 B.C. according to another source.)

Statue of MITHRAS, ancient Persian god of light who was adopted into the Roman pantheon. Shown wearing the Phrygian cap. Louvre, Paris

ORIGINS OF CHRISTIANITY

What do the Dead Sea Scrolls say about Jesus? The short answer: Nothing, and the last of the scrolls have been dated to approximately 68 AD.

The scrolls were discovered in 1948, and the Vatican, after a Church Father was put in charge of the translation, suppressed the publication of the Scrolls for many years.

http://wiki.answers.com/Q/What_do_the_Dead_Sea_Scrolls_say_about_Jesus

" There was no mention of Jesus in the Dead Sea Scrolls because Jesus as a living historical figure, in their theory, did not exist. They could not state that publicly because of the fear of an outcry, but that was the situation. "
(from: http://www.biblemysteries.com/library/james.htm).

Pope Leo X (1513-1521): Some believe that he considered Jesus to be a mere legend.

The Catholic Encyclopedia refers to a widely circulated remark: "How much we and our family have profited by the legend of Christ, is sufficiently evident to all ages."

From: http://www.religioustolerance.org/chr_jcno.htm

EXAMPLE OF RELIGIOUS VIOLENCE- A THIRTY YEAR WAR

There was a 30 year war (1618-1648) over religion
http://en.wikipedia.org/wiki/Thirty_Years'_War

There are wars or conflicts between those who believe in their founder of their religion, but believe differently. In the Middle

East, The Sunni's and the Shia's both treasure their belief in Muhammad, but they often bomb each other, because the other follows a different descendant of Muhammad, or some other different way of belief. The Inquisition (1231? or 1485? to 1835) was about different ways to believe in Jesus Christ and/or different interpretations of the Old or New Testament.

Religions are riddled with intolerance, hate, gender imbalance and therefore I say, it is OK to be a skeptic about all religion, and travel the high road BEYOND ALL RELIGION.

CHRIST NEVER EXISTED

From the last page of the Conclusion of the 701 well documented monumental book, "THE CHRIST SCANDAL" (Stanford House, 2008) by Tony Bushby, who says "Regardless of how many people may be disturbed, there is no religion superior to Truth".

"For people who accept the church's "profitable superstition" (Pope Leo X, d. 1521) without questioning, nothing more can be said; but any enquiring person undertaking the task of simply comparing oldest Bibles with newest Bibles will see how believing Christians were deliberately deceived for sixteen hundred years by men who present themselves as paragons of morality. Over that time, the church effectively created a written devise to instill (sic) and maintain a false belief and used it to preach as true and accurate what it knows is false and fraudulent. Christianity's central doctrines were rendered more dramatic for hoax and profit and reveal nothing proven historically. From beginning to end, the Gospel of Jesus Christ is a work of imaginative fiction that, despite its age, possesses no factual merit and is used by the church as the very essence of its projections. The New Testament is not a unique divine revelation, and if its acknowledged forgeries were deleted, the blood and substance of the Christian religion would go with them.

The church admits that it cannot prove the existence of Jesus Christ [1] and that makes Christianity a farce. In 1514 Pope Leo X called Christ "a fable" [2] and later Pope Paul III expressed similar sentiments, saying that there "was no valid document to demonstrate the existence of Christ" [3]. He confessed that "Jesus never existed", adding that he "was no other than the sun, adored in its Mithraic sect" (Ibid). From that and similar papal pronouncements it is concluded that Jesus Christ was theologically created from premeditated frauds, a plethora of fake and forged documents and books, fictitious Gospels, suppression of early church records [4], mass murder of opponents, [5] (-Think Inquisition-Author) and is sustained today by false claims and a deceptive presentation of the facts.

[1] Catholic Encyclopedia, Pecci Ed., 11, 391-393
[2] Cardinal Bembo, His Letters and Comments on Pope Leo X, Reprint 1842; Also , De Vita Leonis X,
originally published in 1551 (See Entry, Christianity's disbelieving Pope)
[3] Court of Justice, Viterbo, Italy; no 45/b (See Entry, Christ and the Sun)
[4] Encyclopedia Biblica, Adam & Charles Black, London, 1899
[5] See pages numbers in the Index for direction to Entries revealing the true extent of the Inquisition and its agenda.

A SHORT REVIEW OF "THE CHRIST CONSPIRACY"

"The Greatest Story Ever Sold" by Acharya S.
The book is available on Amazon.com, and other retailers.

This book concludes that Christianity is not unique as we believe, but is a rehash of previous myths, a remake if you will, of an amalgamation of other religions. Christianity was created artificially out of other religions to consolidate Roman control over the proliferation of other religions and beliefs.

According to this book, Christ was not a historic figure, but more of a drug to control the masses.

Regarding Biblical Sources : "The story of Jesus Christ can be found only in the forged books of the New Testament, an assortment of gospels and epistles that required many centuries and hands to create."

What about the epistles? "It is clear the epistles do not demonstrate a historical Jesus and are not as early as they are pretended to be, written or edited by a number of hands over several decades during the second century, such that the "historical" Jesus apparently was not even known at that late point.."

What about the Gospels? "Although they are held up by true believers to be the "inspired" stories of the apostles, the canonical gospels were forged at the end of the 2nd century, all four of them probably between 170-180,.." (A.D.-Author)

"There is a reason to believe that both [John and Matthew] were written in the interest of the supremacy of the Church of Rome."

From **Non-Biblical Sources** chapter of the book: "The silence of these historians (non-biblical historians-Author) is, in fact, deafening testimony ....."

Church Father Augustine: .."the eminent Church doctor Augustine readily confessed that Christianity was a rehash of what already existed long prior to the Christian era."

"As Mack says: The narrative gospels can no longer be viewed as the trustworthy accounts of unique and stupendous historical events at the foundation of the Christian faith. The gospels must now be seen as the result of early Christian mythmaking."

"Hilton Hotema declared 'Not one line of the Bible has a known author, and but few incidents of it are corroborated by other testimony."

Acharya, the author, states that Paul, the "Apostle of the Gnostics" did not acknowledge a historic Christ.

Neither did Pope Leo X (1475-1521) making this declaration **"What profit has not that fable of Christ brought us!"**

Acharya says "The fact is that Gnosticism existed first and was eventually changed into orthodox Christianity around 220 CE."

Regarding the Characters in the Christ Conspiracy, Acharya concludes "It is evident that Jesus Christ is a mythical character based on these ubiquitous godmen and universal saviors who were part of the ancient world for thousands of years prior to the Christian era.

The doctrine of turning bread and wine into the body and blood of Christ, found in I Corinthians 10-12 is not original. "This sort of magical ritual was practiced around the world in a variety of forms eons before the Christian era...".

The ancient Mexicans, even before Christianity arrived, believed that by consecrating bread, their priests could turn it into the very body of their god, and by eating it, they would have communion with the deity.

FORGERY IN CHRISTIANITY

http://www.irishoriginsofcivilization.com/irishoriginsexcerpts/oldpage-irishorigins1.html

CONCLUSION OF "THE CHRIST CONSPIRACY, The Greatest Story Ever Sold"

This book says that the Christ myth is the greatest hoax and conspiracy that has ever been perpetrated upon mankind.

"No human culture can survive that bases its fundamental beliefs and perceptions on a hoax, particularly one in which the result has been the endless torture and slaughter of millions around the globe."

This book is a true magnum opus, with copious footnotes by an archaeologist, historian, mythologist, and linguist.

I highly recommend reading this explosive eye-opening book. Review by Samuel Butler-

WHY DID ST. PAUL SAY WOMEN SHOULD NOT SPEAK IN CHURCH AND BE SUBMISSIVE?

King James Bible 1 Corinthians 14:34
"Let your women keep silence in the churches: for it is not permitted unto them to speak; but [they are commanded] to be under obedience, as also saith the law. "

"As in all the congregations of the saints, women should remain silent in the churches. They are not allowed to speak, but must be in submission, as the Law says. If they want to inquire about something, they should ask their own husbands at home; for it is disgraceful for a woman to speak in the church. Did the word of God originate with you? Or are you the only people it has reached?" (1 Cor. 14:33b-36 NIV).

Why did St Paul say that? Why?

The short answer: **HE DIDN'T.** Someone pretending to be Paul said that, lying.

From March 27, 2011 Daily Mail (UK)
See http://preview.tinyurl.com/4fumoaj

SHORT REVIEW OF "JESUS, INTERRUPTED", by Samuel Butler 7/10/2010

Bart D. Ehrman, the author of "Jesus Interrupted, Revealing the Hidden Contradictions in the Bible (and Why We Don't Know About Them") (HarperCollins, 2009) was a fundamentalist evangelical Christian, who was certain that every word in the Bible had been inspired by God when he entered Princeton Theological Seminary, intending to become a Professor of the Bible.

As a seeker of truth, things did not turn out as he planned. He found in historical-critical bible study classes things that biblical scholars have unearthed in the last two hundred years that graduates that even go on to become pastors don't and won't mention in their sermons:

That the authors of the New Testament have diverging views about who Jesus was and how salvation works.

That it contains books that were forged in the name of the apostles by Christian writers who lived decades later.

Established Christian doctrines-such as the suffering messiah, the divinity of Jesus, and the trinity were inventions of still later theologians.

The idea that Jesus was divine was a later Christian invention found only in John, the last gospel, written some 60 years after the events described, and written by an unknown author. The raising of Lazarus from the dead, and the divinity of Jesus are not found in any of the other 3 gospels.

The belief that Jesus was God or divine was not the belief of Jesus's earliest followers, nor of Jesus himself.

Bart D. Ehrman now describes himself as "an agnostic scholar of the New Testament."

SIXTEEN CRUCIFIXIONS BEFORE CHRIST

From: http://www.infidels.org/library/historical/kersey_graves /16/chap16.html

The belief in the crucifixion of Gods was prevalent in various oriental or heathen countries long prior to the reported crucifixion of Christ.

Here are 16:

I. -- CRUCIFIXION OF CHRISHNA OF INDIA, 1200 B.C
II. -- CRUCIFIXION OF THE HINDOO SAKIA, 600 B.C.
III. -- THAMMUZ OF SYRIA CRUCIFIED, 1160 B.C.
IV. -- CRUCIFIXION OF WITTOBA OF THE TELINGONESIC, 552 B.C.
V. -- IAO OF NEPAUL CRUCIFIED, 622 B.C.
VI. -- HESUS OF THE CELTIC DRUIDS CRUCIFIED, 834 B.C.
VII. -- QUEXALCOTE OF MEXICO CRUCIFIED, 587 B.C.
VIII. -- QUIRINUS OF ROME CRUCIFIED, 506 B.C.
IX. -- (AESCHYLUS) PROMETHEUS CRUCIFIED, 547 B.C.
X. -- CRUCIFIXION OF THULIS OF EGYPT, 1700 B.C.
XI. -- CRUCIFIXION OF INDRA OF TIBET, 725 B.C.
XII. -- ALCESTOS OF EURIPIDES CRUCIFIED, 600 B.C.
XIII. -- ATYS OF PHRYGIA CRUCIFIED, 1170 B.C.
XIV. -- CRITE OF CHALDEA CRUCIFIED, 1200 B.C.
XV. -- BALI OF ORISSA CRUCIFIED, 725 B.C.
XVI. -- MITHRA OF PERSIA CRUCIFIED, 600 B.C.

Statement at the end of the above stated web site.

"NOTE. -- The author desires it to be understood with respect to the cases of crucifixion here briefly narrated, that they are not vouched for as actual occurrences, of which there is much ground to doubt. It has neither been his aim or desire to prove them to be real historical events, nor to establish any certain number of cases. Indeed, he deems it unimportant to know, if it could be determined, whether they are fact or fiction, or whether one God was crucified, or many. The moral lesson designed to be taught by this chapter is, simply, that the belief in the crucifixion of Gods was prevalent in various oriental or heathen countries long prior to the reported crucifixion of Christ. If this point is established -- which he feels certain no reader will dispute--then he is not concerned to know whether he has made out sixteen cases of crucifixion or not. Six will prove it as well as sixteen. "

CHRISTIAN CHILD BRIDE

http://www.cbsnews.com/8301-504083_162-5161465-504083.html?tag=contentMain%3bcontentBody

From CBS'S 48 HOURS
July 16, 2009 8:00 AM
Million Dollar Man of God 'Married' 8-Year-Old, Say Feds

TEXARKANA, Ark. (CBS/AP) Evangelist Tony Alamo preyed on his loyal followers' young daughters, once taking a girl as young as eight as his bride and repeatedly sexually assaulting her, a federal prosecutor said Tuesday.

Assistant U.S. Attorney Clay Fowlkes said that girl's story and others unwound an "elaborate facade" Alamo wove around himself.

Lawyers for the 74-year-old Alamo, who is charged with taking underage girls across state lines for sex, argued that the alleged victims traveled across the country to further the outreach and business interests of a "bona fide religious group" that the government targeted out of its own prejudices.

In a number of interviews with the media, Alamo has underscored his belief that, according to the bible, a girl becomes a woman at puberty, no matter how young. He said he also believes that a youngster is permitted to be married if she is able to conceive and deliver a child. But Alamo has denied that his church operates under such terms.

"I am not the one that sets the time," Alamo said in an interview with CNN last year. "That means when a woman is able to conceive and have a child, she is an adult and she could be married."

In the same interview, Alamo also questioned the host, Rick Sanchez, "God inseminated Mary at the age of around 10 to 12. Should we get him for having sex with a young girl?"

When Sanchez asked Alamo why at one point six children were removed from his facility he replied, "They were removed because they just want to make a big deal. They haven't found anything about them. They could check them for 27 hours, or 27 weeks or months or years and they will find out that they are still virgins."

But in court on Tuesday, Fowlkes told jurors that a 15-year-old girl, who left the Alamo ministries in 2006, told the FBI that Alamo married her at age eight. The girl told agents Alamo exchanged wedding vows and rings with her and first sexually assaulted her before she turned 10, Fowlkes said.

From:
http://www.cbsnews.com/stories/2010/04/14/world/main639 7279.shtml?source=related_story&tag=related

PREDATOR PRIESTS SHUFFLED AROUND GLOBE

AP Investigation Found 30 Cases of Priests Accused of Abuse Who Were Transferred or Moved Abroad

In part: There he was, five decades later, the priest who had raped Joe Callander in Massachusetts. The photo in the Roman Catholic newsletter showed him with a smile across his wrinkled face, near-naked Amazon Indian children in his arms and at his feet.

The Rev. Mario Pezzotti was working with children and supervising other priests in Brazil.

It's not an isolated example. In an investigation spanning 21 countries across six continents, The Associated Press found 30 cases of priests accused of abuse who were transferred or moved abroad. Some escaped police investigations. Many had access to children in another country, and some abused again.

A priest who admitted to abuse in Los Angeles went to the Philippines, where U.S. church officials mailed him checks and advised him not to reveal their source. A priest in Canada was convicted of sexual abuse and then moved to France, where he was convicted of abuse again in 2005. Another priest was moved back and forth between Ireland and England, despite being diagnosed as a pederast, a man who commits sodomy with boys.

"The pattern is if a priest gets into trouble and it's close to becoming a scandal or if the law might get involved, they send them to the missions abroad," said Richard Sipe, a former Benedictine monk and critic of what he says is a practice of international transfers of accused and admitted priest child abusers. "Anything to avoid a scandal."

You may be interested in the following lengthy list of Bible verses compiled and paraphrased by renowned freethinker Barbara G. Walker:

http://tinyurl.com/7uud77e
Sent to me from Acharya S. (http://TruthBeKnown.com/)

BIBLE MORALITY OR DEPRAVITY

(Following are biblical verses compiled by independent comparative religion scholar and Freethought Nation guestwriter Barbara G. Walker, concerning the supposed "morality" of the Bible. The paraphrases and commentary are Barbara's, while the original verses are linked. For more of Barbara's Bible investigations, see MAN MADE GOD, especially the section on Bible Studies.)

For the verses without paraphrases and commentary, please go here: http://tinyurl.com/7uud77e and click on the Bible verse.

BIBLE MORALITY (King James Version)

Compiled by Barbara G. Walker, author of Man Made God, et al.

1. KILLING. (AS IN "THOU SHALT NOT"...???)

The biblical god personally kills a total of 371,186 people, not counting his slaughter of every living thing in Genesis 7. The biblical god also orders the killing of a total of 1,862,265.

Gen 22:2 - God accepts human sacrifices (including that of Jesus, later).
Ex 12:29 - God kills all the firstborn in the land of Egypt.
Ex 15:3 - God is a god of war.
Ex 21:15, 17 - Anyone who strikes or curses a parent must be killed.
Ex 22:18 - Every witch must be killed.
Ex 22:19, 20 - You must kill anyone who "lieth with a beast," or who worships any god other than Yahweh.
Ex 31:15 - Anyone who works on the Sabbath must be killed.

Lev 20:10, 13, 27 - You must kill adulterers, homosexuals, wizards and spirit mediums.

Lev 21:9 - Any priest's daughter who fornicates must be burned alive.

Lev 24:16 - Blasphemers must be killed.

Num 16:27-33 - God caused the whole tribe of Korah -- men, women, and children -- to be buried alive.

Num 21:3 - God caused the destruction of all the Canaanites.

Num 31:7-35 - God orders Moses to kill the Midianites, making sure to slaughter not only the men but also the boys and females, except for the 32,000 virgin girls.

Deut 3:4 - God is pleased that his warriors destroyed 60 cities.

Deut 7:16 - You must kill all the people God delivers into your hands, and "thine eye shall have no pity upon them."

Deut 13:5 - Any prophet or "dreamer of dreams," who serves another god, must be killed.

Deut 13:6-9 - If your brother, son, daughter, wife, or friend tempts you to worship other gods, "thou shalt surely kill him."

Deut 13:13-15 - If the people of any city worship other gods, you must slaughter them all, including their cattle.

Deut 17:5 - Any man or woman who worships other deities of sun, moon or stars must be stoned to death.

Deut 18:20 - False prophets must be killed.

Deut 20:16-17 - God commands complete destruction of all Hittites, Amorites, Canaanites, Perizzites, Hivites and Jebusites, and "thou shalt save alive nothing that breatheth."

Deut 22:21 - A bride found not to be a virgin must be stoned to death.

Deut 22:22 - Adulterers must be killed.

Deut 22:23-24 - A girl who is raped within city limits, and fails to cry out, must be killed.

Deut 28:22-28 - If you don't obey God's commandments, he will punish you with consumption, fever, extreme burning, blasting, mildew, hemorrhoids, the scab, the itch, the botch of Egypt, etc., as well as "madness, and blindness, and astonishment of heart."

Josh 6:21 - God's warriors destroyed Jericho and killed every man, woman, child, and domestic animal.

Josh 8:25 - God's warriors killed 12,000 people in the city of Ai.

Josh 19:47 - The children of Dan wanted more room, so they destroyed the whole population of Leshen and took their territory.

Judges 1:17-18 - Judah and Simeon utterly destroyed the populations of Zephath, Gaza, Askelon and Ekron.

Judges 11:39 - In accord with God's law, Jephthah was forced to burn his virgin daughter to death as a sacrifice.

Judges 15:15 - God enables Samson to kill 1,000 men with the jawbone of an ass.

Judges 20:46 - At Gibeah, Benjamin's men killed 25,000 people and burned every town.

1 Sam 6:19 - God kills 50,070 people for trying to peek into the Ark.

1 Sam 15:3 - God commands the destruction of Amalek: "Slay both men and women, infant and suckling, ox and sheep, camel and ass."

2 Sam 6:7 - God kills Uzzah for touching the Ark, even though he was trying to save it from falling off its oxcart.

1 Kings 18:40 - God commands the slaughter of "prophets of Baal".

1 Kings 20:36 - Because a man didn't "obey the voice of the Lord," a lion was sent to kill him.

2 Kings 2:24 - God sent bears to tear apart 42 children for making fun of Elisha's bald head.

2 Kings 10:25 - God commands the killing of a multitude in the temple of Baal.

2 Kings 19:35 - God's angel killed 185,000 Assyrians in a single night.

1 Chron 21:14 - God kills 70,000 Israelites with a pestilence.

2 Chron 15:13 - Any man or woman who refuses to "seek the Lord God of Israel" must be killed.

Job 1:15-19 - God arranges the killing of Job's children, servants and animals.

Isa 13:16 - God promises that all the Babylonians' children will be "dashed to pieces before their eyes;" their wives will be raped.

Isa 45:7 - God says "I create evil."

Jer 48:10 - Killing for God is mandatory; God curses anyone who "keepeth back his sword from blood."

Jer 50:21 - God commands that the people of Merathaim and Pekod be "utterly destroyed."

Ezek 9:5-7 - God calls for purging in Jerusalem: "let not your eye spare, neither have ye pity: slay utterly old and young, both maids and little children, and women... fill the courts with the slain."

Ezek 35:8 - God promises to fill the mountains, hills, valleys and rivers with slain men.

Hosea 13:16 - God promises to have Samaritan infants dashed to pieces, and pregnant women will have their bellies slashed open.

Nahum 1:2 - God is jealous, full of vengeance and wrath.

Zeph 1:3 - God threatens to destroy everything, man and beast, birds and fishes.

Zeph 1:18 - "The whole land shall be devoured by the fire of his jealousy."

Zeph 3:6 - God brags that he has destroyed many nations.

Zech 13:3 - A false prophet must be killed by his father and mother.

2. RAPE

Ex 21:7-8 - A father may sell his daughter to be a "maidservant" (or sex slave) who must "please her master."

Num 31:7, 18 - God orders his warriors to kill every living thing in a captured city, except the virgin girls, who are to be raped and turned into sex slaves.

Deut 21:11-12 - If a warrior likes the look of a female war captive, he can take her to be one of his "wives."

Deut 22:28-29 - A man who rapes a virgin may take her for a wife if he pays her father 50 shekels of silver. (Yet, a bride found not to be a virgin must be stoned to death - Deut 22:20-21).

Judges 5:30 - The spoils of war include "a damsel or two" for every man.

Judges 21:12-23 - God's warriors killed all the inhabitants of Jabeshgilead except for 400 virgin girls, who were taken as slaves. If there are not enough girls to go around, God's warriors may raid neighboring towns for more to rape.

3. SLAVERY

Gen 9:25 - God cursed Ham, son of Noah, with perpetual slavery for the crime of seeing his father naked. (Ham was formerly considered the ancestor of all "blacks.")

Ex 21:4 - A male slave may marry and have children, and may go free after six years; but his family remains the property (or hostages?) of his master.

Ex 21:7 - A man may sell his daughter as a sex slave.

Ex 21:20-21 - A man may be punished for beating a male or female slave to death, but if the victim survives the beating for a few days, then there is no penalty.

Lev 19:20 - When a man has sex with a female slave (or "bondmaid"), SHE must be scourged.

Eph 6:5 - Paul says slaves must obey their masters "with fear and trembling."

Titus 2:9 - Paul says slaves must obey and please their masters.

1 Tim 6:1 - Paul says slaves must "count their masters worthy of all honor."

4. WAS JESUS ETHICAL?

Matt 5:28-32 - Jesus says marriage to a divorcee is adultery; and a man who ogles a woman has already committed adultery; and that you must cut off your hand or pluck out your eye if it offends.

Matt 6:19-34 - Jesus says don't save any money and don't plan ahead.

Matt 8:32 - Having no regard for private property, Jesus destroys a herd of someone else's pigs.

Matt 10:34 - Jesus says he brings not peace on earth but "a sword."

Matt 19:12 - Jesus says the best way for a man to be sure of getting into heaven is to have himself castrated.

Mark 11:13 - Jesus destroys a fig tree for not bearing figs out of season.

Mark 14:4-7 - Jesus says it is more important to anoint him with precious ointment than to give to the poor, who will always be here. (Why not just get rid of poverty?)

Mark 16:18 - Jesus says anyone who believes in him can play with venomous snakes or drink poison without harm. (This act has been often tried, with rather unsatisfactory results.)

Luke 12:47-48 - Jesus says it is permissible to whip slaves.

Luke 14:26 - Jesus says no man can be his disciple unless he hates his parents, siblings, wife, children, and himself as well.

Luke 19:27 - In telling a parable, Jesus insinuates that anyone who denies his rulership must be killed.

John 15:6 - Jesus says anyone who doesn't believe in him must be burned.

Acts 5:5-10 - Ananias and his wife Sapphira were killed for withholding money from the church.

2 John 1:10-11 - A Christian is forbidden to offer hospitality to a non-Christian, not even to wish him "Godspeed" on parting.

5. WOMEN IN THE NEW TESTAMENT

1 Cor 11:3-10 - Women are inferior "because man was not created for woman, but woman was created for man." Every woman "while praying or prophesying" must have her head covered "because of the angels," meaning the spirits (it used to be believed that women's hair attracts spirits).

1 Cor 14:34-35 - Women must not speak in church, which is a shame for them to do. If they want to ask questions, they must learn from their husbands at home.

Eph 5:22 - Wives must submit to their husbands as they would to God.

1 Tim 2:11-15 - A woman must not teach, or hold authority over a man, but must "learn in silence with all subjection," because "Adam was not deceived, but the woman being deceived was in the transgression." (So, being gullible is the original sin.)

1 Tim 5:9 - Paul says the only women acceptable by the council of elders are devout, monogamous women over the age of sixty.

6. SILLINESS

Gen 1:11-19 - God made all green plants on the third day of creation, but neglected to supply the sun (on which both plants and "days" depend) until the fourth day.

Gen 6:6-7 - Because a few people displeased him, God "repented" having made the world, and decided to destroy all life on earth.

Lev 11:5-6 - God thinks rabbits are cud-chewing animals.

Deut 22:5 - All cross-dressers, or women who wear pants, are "abominations."

Deut 25:11-12 - A woman who seizes a man's genitals, even to defend her husband from an attacker, must have her hand cut off.

Deut 33:17 - God believes in unicorns.

Matt 5:22 - Jesus says anyone who calls another "fool" will go to hell, but then he does it himself (Matt 23:17).

1 Tim 2:9 - Christian women are forbidden to braid their hair or wear jewelry.

James 5:14-15 - Prayer by the elders of the church is the only sure cure for sickness. (Christian Science, anyone?)

End of Barbara G. Walker compilation.

OLD TESTAMENT

Exodus 2:
[11]And it came to pass in those days, when Moses was grown, that he went out unto his brethren, and looked on their burdens: and he spied an Egyptian smiting an Hebrew, one of his brethren.

[12]And he looked this way and that way, and when he saw that there was no man, he slew the Egyptian, and hid him in the sand.

Genocide in the Old Testament:

Now **go and smite Amalek** (a nomadic nation south of Palestine-Author)**, and utterly destroy all that they have, and spare them not; but slay both man and woman, infant and suckling, ox and sheep, camel and ass.** 1 Samuel 15:3
God commanding Moses to kill:

"They fought against Midian, as **the LORD commanded Moses, and killed every man........Now kill all the boys [innocent kids]. And kill every woman who has slept with a man,** but save for yourselves every girl who has never slept with a man. (Numbers 31:7,17-18)"

Kill everything that "breathes" from humans and animals!
Deuteronomy 20:16

However, in the cities of the nations the Lord your God is giving you as an inheritance, **do not leave alive anything that breathes.**

Speaking of Moses:
How about this:

MOSES NEVER EXISTED

There is no evidence for the existence of Moses. Although he is portrayed as an influential member of the Egyptian royal household, he is not mentioned in any Egyptian record. Nor is there any evidence to support the idea that the Jews were ever held captive in Egypt or that they made an exodus from the country under Moses' command. The Egyptians chronicled their history in great detail but make no mention of any captive Jews. Amongst the hundreds of thousands of Egyptian monumental inscriptions, tomb inscriptions and papyri, there is complete silence about the '600,000 men on foot, besides women and children' who The Book of Exodus tells us escaped from Pharaoh's armies.

The story of Moses, with its many miracles, has all the hallmarks of a myth. The account of Moses' birth is a retelling of the myth of the birth of Sargon the Great, the king of Akkad, which is known in a number of variations from the early sixth century BCE. Like Moses, the child Sargon is 'set in a basket of rushes' and 'cast into the river', from which he is later rescued by an influential woman. Similar Greek stories tell of the child Dionysus confined in a chest and thrown into the river Nile. These probably all go back to Egyptian stories which tell of Osiris confined in a chest and thrown in the Nile.

ABRAHAM

Abraham is considered to be the great patriarch of the Jewish nation. He is also an important figure for Christians and Muslims. Evidence for his existence is crucial to the idea that these three religions might all be 'Sons of Abraham', as is often claimed. According to Biblical chronology Abraham moved to Canaan about 2100 BCE. But this is impossible as Abraham is said to have come from the Chaldean city of Ur that did not exist until after 1000 BCE. Prior to this date there were no Chaldeans. Genesis tells us that Abraham's son Isaac sought help from Abimelech, the king of the Philistines, yet the Philistines were not a presence in the area until after 1200 BCE. And although the camel is mentioned frequently in the stories of Abraham and the other patriarchs, the domestication of the camel did not happen until around 1000 BCE. The camel caravan described frequently in the Tanakh (Old Testament-author), with its cargo of 'gum, balm, and myrrh', did not become widespread until the eighth century BCE.

And this:

Originally published in 1999 in Ha'aretz magazine and then reprinted in the Biblical Archaeological Review, an article written by a Jewish professor at Tel Aviv University seeks to undermine biblical faith by denying the historicity of the patriarchs. The attack is cleverly disguised as pure science, but in truth it is only academic arrogance. Professor Herzog expresses in the article his frustration that his people (the Jews) refuse to accept his "scientific" conclusions. The rejection is not surprising, considering that the professor attempted to demolish 4,000 years of Jewish (and Christian) history. Note the introductory summary of the article:

Following 70 years of intensive excavations in the Land of Israel, archaeologists have found out: The patriarchs' acts are legendary stories, we did not sojourn in Egypt or make an exodus, we did not conquer the land. Neither is there any mention of the empire of David and Solomon (Herzog, 1999). [4]

From "The Holy Bible, from the Ancient Eastern Text, Goerge M. Lamsa's Translation of the Peshitta"

Psalm 137:9
Blessed shall be who takes and dashes your little ones against
the stones.

"From http://www.humanistsofutah.org/2002/WhyCantIOwnA
Canadian_10-02.html (In English)

WHY CAN'T I OWN A CANADIAN?

October 2002
Dr. Laura Schlessinger is a radio personality who dispenses advice to people who call in to her radio show. Recently, she said that, as an observant Orthodox Jew, homosexuality is an abomination according to Leviticus 18:22 and cannot be condoned under any circumstance. The following is an open letter to Dr. Laura penned by an east coast resident, which was posted on the Internet. It's funny, as well as informative:

Dear Dr. Laura:

Thank you for doing so much to educate people regarding God's Law. I have learned a great deal from your show, and try to share that knowledge with as many people as I can. When someone tries to defend the homosexual lifestyle, for example, I simply remind them that Leviticus 18:22 clearly states it to be an abomination. End of debate. I do need some advice from you, however, regarding some of the other specific laws and how to follow them:

When I burn a bull on the altar as a sacrifice, I know it creates a pleasing odor for the Lord - Lev.1:9. The problem is my neighbors. They claim the odor is not pleasing to them. Should I smite them?

I would like to sell my daughter into slavery, as sanctioned in Exodus 21:7. In this day and age, what do you think would be a fair price for her?

I know that I am allowed no contact with a woman while she is in her period of menstrual uncleanliness - Lev.15:19- 24. The problem is, how do I tell? I have tried asking, but most women take offense.

Lev. 25:44 states that I may indeed possess slaves, both male and female, provided they are purchased from neighboring nations. A friend of mine claims that this applies to Mexicans, but not Canadians. Can you clarify? Why can't I own Canadians?

I have a neighbor who insists on working on the Sabbath. Exodus 35:2 clearly states he should be put to death. Am I morally obligated to kill him myself?

A friend of mine feels that even though eating shellfish is an abomination - Lev. 11:10, it is a lesser abomination than homosexuality. I don't agree. Can you settle this?

Lev. 21:20 states that I may not approach the altar of God if I have a defect in my sight. I have to admit that I wear reading glasses. Does my vision have to be 20/20, or is there some wiggle room here?

Most of my male friends get their hair trimmed, including the hair around their temples, even though this is expressly forbidden by Lev. 19:27. How should they die?

I know from Lev. 11:6-8 that touching the skin of a dead pig makes me unclean, but may I still play football if I wear gloves?

My uncle has a farm. He violates Lev. 19:19 by planting two different crops in the same field, as does his wife by wearing garments made of two different kinds of thread (cotton/polyester blend). He also tends to curse and blaspheme a lot. Is it really necessary that we go to all the trouble of getting the whole town together to stone them? - Lev.24:10-16. Couldn't we just burn them to death at a private family affair like we do with people who sleep with their in-laws? (Lev. 20:14)

I know you have studied these things extensively, so I am confident you can help. Thank you again for reminding us that God's word is eternal and unchanging."

JEWISH TRADITIONAL RELIGION

The below is from :
http://www.truthtellers.org/alerts/pedophiliasecret.html

This is what I got when I did a search on "Babylonian Talmud" and a couple of other key words.

In the late 19th century, most European Jews were a people of the book. But their book wasn't the Bible. It was the Babylonian Talmud. To this day, the Talmud remains Judaism's highest moral, ethical and legal authority.

What's the difference between the Torah, Talmud, and Pentatuch?

From:
http://answers.yahoo.com/question/index?qid=201004201305 13AAsrAM6

The Pentateuch is the Torah, or rather it's the Christian version of the Torah. The first five books of the Hebrew Bible (Tanakh is the Jewish version, Old Testament is the Christian version). There are differences in the versions, translation differences and ordering, which give a different message.

The Talmud is different. It includes commentary on the law, including debates. It's central to rabbinical (modern) Judaism.

HOW ABOUT THIS FOR HATE?

Genocide Advocated by the Talmud
Minor Tractates. Soferim 15, Rule 10. This is the saying of Rabbi Simon ben Yohai: Tob shebe goyyim harog ("Even the best of the gentiles should all be killed").

This passage is from the original Hebrew of the Babylonian Talmud as quoted by the 1907 Jewish Encyclopedia, published by Funk and Wagnalls and compiled by Isidore Singer, under the entry, "Gentile," (p. 617).

Israelis annually take part in a national pilgrimage to the grave of Simon ben Yohai, to honor this rabbi who advocated the extermination of non-Jews. (Jewish Press, June 9, 1989, p. 56B).

Apologists say this ("Even the best of the gentiles should all be killed") only applies in a Jewish war.

Well, it DID come up in the 1973 Yom Kippur war:

Short answer: It is OK to kill civilian women and children in a war involving Israel [8]:

Excerpts:

Letter from the soldier Moshe to Rabbi Shim'on Weiser:

With God's help, to His Honor, my dear Rabbi, 'First I would like to ask how you and your family are. I hope all is well. I am, thank God, feeling well. A long time I have not written. Please forgive me. Sometimes I recall the verse "when shall I come and appear before God?' I hope, without being certain, that I shall come during one of the leaves. I must do so.

'In one of the discussions in our group, there was a debate about the "purity of weapons" and we discussed whether it is permitted to kill unarmed men - or women and children? Or perhaps we should take revenge on the Arabs? And then everyone answered according to his own understanding. I could not arrive at a clear decision, whether Arabs should be treated like the Amalekites, meaning that one is permitted to murder [sic] them until their remembrance is blotted out from under heaven, or perhaps one should do as in a just war, in which one kills only the soldiers?

'A second problem I have is whether I am permitted to put myself in danger by allowing a woman to stay alive? For there have been cases when women threw hand grenades. Or am I permitted to give water to an Arab who put his hand up? For there may be reason to fear that he only means to deceive me and will kill me, and such things have happened.

'I conclude with a warm greeting to the rabbi and all his family. - Moshe.'

Reply of (Rabbi) Shim'on Weiser to Moshe:

'With the help of Heaven. Dear Moshe, Greetings.

'I am starting this letter this evening although I know I cannot finish it this evening, both because I am busy and because I would like to make it a long letter, to answer your questions in full, for which purpose I shall have to copy out some of the sayings of our sages, of blessed memory, and interpret them.

'The non-Jewish nations have a custom according to which war has its own rules, like those of a game, like the rules of football or basketball. But according to the sayings of our sages, of blessed memory, [...] war for us is not a game but a vital necessity, and only by this standard must we decide how to wage it. On the one hand [...] we seem to learn that if a Jew murders a Gentile, he is regarded as a murderer and, except for the fact that no court has the right to punish him, the gravity of the deed is like that of any other murder. But we find in the very same authorities in another place [...] that Rabbi Shim'on used to say: "The best of Gentiles - kill him; the best of snakes dash out its brains."

'It might perhaps be argued that the expression "kill" in the saying of R. Shim'on is only figurative and should not be taken literally but as meaning "oppress" or some similar attitude, and in this way we also avoid a contradiction with the authorities quoted earlier. Or one might argue that this saying, though meant literally, is [merely] his own personal opinion, disputed by other sages [quoted earlier]. But we find the true explanation in the Tosalot. There [....] we learn the following comment on the talmudic pronouncement that Gentiles who fall into a well should not be helped out, but neither should they be pushed into the well to be killed, which means that they should neither be saved from death nor killed directly. And the Tosafot write as follows:

"And if it is queried [because] in another place it was said The best of Gentiles - kill him, then the answer is that this [saying] is meant for wartime." [...]

'According to the commentators of the Tosafot, a distinction must be made between wartime and peace, so that although during peace time it is forbidden to kill Gentiles, in a case that occurs in wartime it is a mitzvah [imperative, religious duty] to kill them. [...]

'And this is the difference between a Jew and a Gentile: although the rule "Whoever comes to kill you, kill him first", applies to a Jew, as was said in Tractate Sanhedrin [of the Talmud], page 72a, still it only applies to him if there is [actual] ground to fear that he is coming to kill you. But a Gentile during wartime is usually to be presumed so, except when it is quite clear that he has no evil intent. This is the rule of "purity of weapons" according to the Halakhah - and not the alien conception which is now accepted in the Israeli army and which has been the cause of many [Jewish] casualties. I enclose a newspaper cutting with the speech made last week in the Knesset by Rabbi Kalman Kahana, which shows in a very lifelike - and also painful - way how this "purity of weapons" has caused deaths.

'I conclude here, hoping that you will not find the length of this letter irksome. This subject was being discussed even without your letter, but your letter caused me to write up the whole matter.

'Be in peace, you and all Jews, and [I hope to] see you soon, as you say. Yours - Shim'on.

Reply of Moshe to R. (Rabbi) Shim'on Weiser:

'To His Honor, my dear Rabbi,

'First I hope that you and your family are in health and are all right.

'I have received your long letter and am grateful for your personal watch over me, for I assume that you write to many, and most of your time is taken up with your studies in your own program.

'Therefore my thanks to you are doubly deep.

'As for the letter itself, I have understood it as follows:

'In wartime I am not merely permitted, but enjoined to kill every Arab man and woman whom I chance upon, if there is reason to fear that they help in the war against us, directly or indirectly. And as far as I am concerned I have to kill them even if that might result in an involvement with the military law. I think that this matter of the purity of weapons should be transmitted to educational institutions, at least the religious ones, so that they should have a position about this subject and so that they will not wander in the broad fields of "logic", especially on this subject; and the rule has to be explained as it should be followed in practice. For, I am sorry to say, I have seen different types of "logic" here even among the religious comrades. I do hope that you shall be active in this, so that our boys will know the line of their ancestors clearly and unambiguously.

'I conclude here, hoping that when the [training] course ends, in about a month, I shall be able to come to the yeshivah[talmudic college]. Greetings - Moshe.'

As for Gentiles, the basic talmudic principle is that their lives must not be saved, although it is also forbidden to murder them outright. The Talmud itself expresses this in the maxim 'Gentiles are neither to be lifted [out of a well] nor hauled down [into it]'. Maimonides explains:

"As for Gentiles with whom we are not at war ... their death must not be caused, but it is forbidden to save them if they are at the point of death; if, for example, one of them is seen falling into the sea, he should not be rescued, for it is written: 'neither shalt thou stand against the blood of thy fellow" - but [a Gentile] is not thy fellow."

In particular, a Jewish doctor must not treat a Gentile patient. Maimonides - himself an illustrious physician - is quite explicit on this. in another passage he repeats the distinction between 'thy fellow' and a Gentile, and concludes: 'and from this learn ye, that it is forbidden to heal a Gentile even for payment...'

However, the refusal of a Jew - particularly a Jewish doctor - to save the life of a Gentile may, if it becomes known, antagonize powerful Gentiles and so put Jews in danger. Where such danger exists, the obligation to avert it supersedes the ban on helping the Gentile. Thus Maimonides continues: ' ... but if you fear him or his hostility, cure him for payment, though you are forbidden to do so without payment.' In fact, Maimonides himself was Saladin's (Sultan of Egypt and Syria, and captor of Jerusalem and of Richard the Lionhearted) personal physician. (Saladin died-1193-of a short illness. Hmmm ⁇. Author). His insistence on demanding payment - presumably in order to make sure that the act is not one of human charity but an unavoidable duty - is however not absolute. For in another passage he allows Gentile whose hostility is feared to be treated 'even gratis, if it is unavoidable'. [8]

You don't think the Talmudic scriptures influence current beliefs? Think again:

On Purim, Feb. 25, 1994, Israeli army officer Baruch Goldstein, an orthodox Jew from Brooklyn, massacred 40 Palestinian civilians, including children, while they knelt in prayer in a mosque. Goldstein was a disciple of the late Brooklyn Rabbi Meir Kahane, who told CBS News that his teaching that Arabs are "dogs" is derived "from the Talmud." (CBS 60 Minutes, "Kahane").

University of Jerusalem Prof. Ehud Sprinzak described Kahane and Goldstein's philosophy: "They believe it's God's will that they commit violence against goyim, a Hebrew term for non-Jews." (NY Daily News, Feb. 26, 1994, p. 5).

Rabbi Yitzhak Ginsburg declared, "We have to recognize that Jewish blood and the blood of a goy are not the same thing." (NY Times, June 6, 1989, p.5).

Rabbi Yaacov Perrin said, "One million Arabs are not worth a Jewish fingernail." (NY Daily News, Feb. 28, 1994, p.6).

Does the Talmud share Christianity's foundation of wholesome moral values? Hardly. Instead, the Talmud is the sleazy substrata of a religious system gone terribly astray; it is that code of Pharisaic unbelief Christ described as "full of all uncleanness" (Matt. 23:27).

Shockingly, Judaism's most revered authority actually endorses such one of the greatest sins of all: child molestation.

I am open to the below statements and other claims herein being "debunked". There is a lot of disinformation out there. In other words I am open to this purported history being proven wrong-Author

THREE YEAR OLD BRIDES

When Christ accused the Pharisees of His day of being Satan's spiritual children, He fully realized what they were capable of. second century Rabbi Simeon ben Yohai, one of Judaism's very greatest rabbis and a creator of Kabbalah, sanctioned pedophilia—permitting molestation of baby girls even younger than three! He proclaimed, "A proselyte who is under the age of three years and a day is permitted to marry a priest." [5] Subsequent rabbis refer to ben Yohai's endorsement of pedophilia as "halakah," (In Judaism, all laws and ordinances evolved since biblical times to regulate worship and the daily lives of the Jewish people) or binding Jewish law. [3] Has ben Yohai, child rape advocate, been disowned by modern Jews? Hardly. Today, in ben Yohai's hometown of Meron, Israel, tens of thousands of orthodox and ultra-orthodox Jews gather annually for days and nights of singing and dancing in his memory.

References to pedophilia abound in the Talmud. They occupy considerable sections of Treatises Kethuboth and Yebamoth and are enthusiastically endorsed by the Talmud's definitive legal work, Treatise Sanhedrin. The Pharisees Endorsed Child Sex.

The rabbis of the Talmud are notorious for their legal hairsplitting, and quibbling debates. But they share rare agreement about their right to molest three year old girls. In contrast to many hotly debated issues, hardly a hint of dissent rises against the prevailing opinion (expressed in many clear passages) that pedophilia is not only normal but scriptural as well! It's as if the rabbis have found an exalted truth whose majesty silences debate.

Because the Talmudic authorities who sanction pedophilia are so renowned, and because pedophilia as "halakah" is so explicitly emphasized, not even the translators of the Soncino edition of the Talmud (1936) dared insert a footnote suggesting the slightest criticism. They only comment: "Marriage, of course, was then at a far earlier age than now." [5]

In fact, footnote 5 to Sanhedrin 60b rejects the right of a Talmudic rabbi to disagree with ben Yohai's endorsement of pedophilia: "How could they [the rabbis], contrary to the opinion of R. Simeon ben Yohai, which has scriptural support, forbid the marriage of the young proselyte?" [5]

OUT OF BABYLON

It was in Babylon after the exile under Nebuchadnezzar in 597 BC that Judaism's leading sages probably began to indulge in pedophilia. Babylon was the staggeringly immoral capitol of the ancient world. For 1600 years, the world's largest population of Jews flourished within it.

As an example of their evil, Babylonian priests said a man's religious duty included regular sex with temple prostitutes. Bestiality was widely tolerated. So Babylonians hardly cared whether a rabbi married a three year old girl.

But with expulsion of the Jews in the 11th century AD, mostly to western Christian lands, Gentile tolerance of Jewish pedophilia abruptly ended.

Still, a shocking contradiction lingers: If Jews want to revere the transcendent wisdom and moral guidance of the Pharisees and their Talmud, they must accept the right of their greatest ancient sages to violate children. To this hour, no synod of Judaism has repudiated their vile practice. [5]

SEX WITH A "MINOR" PERMITTED

What exactly did these sages say?

The Pharisees justified child rape by explaining that a boy of nine years was not a "man" (See, "Judaism and Homosexuality: A Marriage Made in Hell") Thus they exempted him from God's Mosaic Law: "You shall not lie with a male as one lies with a female; it is an abomination" (Lev. 18:22) One passage in the Talmud gives permission for a woman who molested her young son to marry a high priest. It concludes, "All agree that the connection of a boy aged nine years and a day is a real connection; whilst that of one less than eight years is not." Because a boy under 9 is sexually immature, he can't "throw guilt" on the active offender, morally or legally.

A woman could molest a young boy without questions of morality even being raised: "...the intercourse of a small boy is not regarded as a sexual act." The Talmud also says, "A male aged nine years and a day who cohabits with his deceased brother's wife acquires her (as wife)." Clearly, the Talmud teaches that a woman is permitted to marry and have sex with a nine year old boy. [6]

SEX AT THREE YEARS AND ONE DAY

In contrast to Simeon ben Yohai's dictum that sex with a little girl is permitted under the age of three years, the general teaching of the Talmud is that the rabbi must wait until a day after her third birthday. She could be taken in marriage simply by the act of rape.

R. Joseph said: Come and hear! A maiden aged three years and a day may be acquired in marriage by coition and if her deceased husband's brother cohabits with her, she becomes his. (Sanhedrin 55b)

The example of Phineas, a priest, himself marrying an underage virgin of three years is considered by the Talmud as proof that such infants are "fit for cohabitation."

The Talmud teaches that an adult woman's molestation of a nine year old boy is "not a sexual act" and cannot "throw guilt" upon her because the little boy is not truly a "man." But they use opposite logic to sanction rape of little girls aged three years and one day: Such infants they count as "women," sexually mature and fully responsible to comply with the requirements of marriage.

The Talmud footnotes 3 and 4 to Sanhedrin 55a clearly tell us when the rabbis considered a boy and girl sexually mature and thus ready for marriage. "At nine years a male attains sexual matureness... The sexual matureness of woman is reached at the age of three." No Rights for Child Victims.

The Pharisees were hardly ignorant of the trauma felt by molested children. To complicate redress, the Talmud says a rape victim must wait until she was of age before there would be any possibility of restitution. She must prove that she lived and would live as a devoted Jewess, and she must protest the loss of her virginity on the very hour she comes of age. "As soon as she was of age one hour and did not protest she cannot protest anymore." [7] The Talmud defends these strict measures as necessary to forestall the possibility of a Gentile child bride rebelling against Judaism and spending the damages awarded to her as a heathen - an unthinkable blasphemy! But the rights of the little girl were really of no great consequence, for, "When a grown-up man has intercourse with a little girl it is nothing, for when the girl is less than this (three years and a day) it is as if one put the finger into the eye." The footnote says that as "tears come to the eye again and again, so does virginity come back to the little girl under three years." [7]

In most cases, the Talmud affirms the innocence of male and female victims of pedophilia. Defenders of the Talmud claim this proves the Talmud's amazing moral advancement and benevolence toward children; they say it contrasts favorably with "primitive" societies where the child would have been stoned along with the adult perpetrator.

Actually, the rabbis, from self-protection, were intent on proving the innocence of both parties involved in pedophilia: the child, but more importantly, the pedophile. They stripped a little boy of his right to "throw guilt" on his assailant and demanded complicity in sex from a little girl. By thus providing no significant moral or legal recourse for the child, the Talmud clearly reveals whose side it is on: the raping rabbi.

Pedophilia Widespread Child rape was practiced in the highest circles of Judaism. This is illustrated from Yebamoth 60b:

There was a certain town in the land of Israel the legitimacy of whose inhabitants was disputed, and Rabbi sent R. Romanos who conducted an inquiry and found in it the daughter of a proselyte who was under the age of three years and one day, and Rabbi declared her eligible to live with a priest.

The footnote says that she was "married to a priest" and the rabbi simply permitted her to live with her husband, thus upholding "halakah" as well as the dictum of Simeon ben Yohai, "A proselyte who is under the age of three years and one day is permitted to marry a priest."

These child brides were expected to submit willingly to sex. Yeb. 12b confirms that under eleven years and one day a little girl is not permitted to use a contraceptive but "must carry on her marital intercourse in the usual manner."

In Sanhedrin 76b a blessing is given to the man who marries off his children before they reach the age of puberty, with a contrasting curse on anyone who waits longer. In fact, failure to have married off one's daughter by the time she is 12-1/2, the Talmud says, is as bad as one who "returns a lost article to a Cuthean" (Gentile) - a deed for which "the Lord will not spare him." This passage says: "... it is meritorious to marry off one's children whilst minors." The mind reels at the damage to the untold numbers of girls who were sexually abused within Judaism during the heyday of pedophilia. Such child abuse, definitely practiced in the second century, continued, at least in Babylon, for another 900 years.

The above is from
http://www.truthtellers.org/alerts/pedophiliasecret.html
I had never heard of this site before, but it confirms other information that I have discovered from other sources.

ISLAM

These say a Muslim should kill unbelievers (unless they repent and give to charity) (Muhammad was well known for asking for "tribute"-author).

Koran: Sura **9:5** But when the forbidden months are past, then fight and slay the Pagans (non-believers-like Christians and Jews-author) wherever ye find them, and seize them, beleaguer them, and lie in wait for them in every stratagem (of war); but if they repent, and establish regular prayers and practise regular charity, then open the way for them: for Allah is Oft-forgiving, Most Merciful.

That is like when the Christians strung up natives by their wrists or fingers, and only letting them down if they accepted Christianity.

Unbelievers are beasts to be hated:

Sura **8:55** "For the worst of beasts in the sight of Allah are those who reject Him: They will not believe."
Sura **9:123** O ye who believe! fight the unbelievers who gird you about, and let them find firmness in you: and know that Allah is with those who fear Him.
If you believe in Allah, do not love anyone who is an un-believer, even if it is your father or brother;
Sura **58:22** Thou wilt not find any people who believe in Allah and the Last Day, loving those who resist Allah and His Apostle,

even though they were their fathers or their sons, or their brothers, or their kindred.
Hadith 4363:

From Wikipedia: A hadith was originally an oral tradition relevant to the actions and customs of the Islamic prophet Muhammad.
I shall cast terror into the hearts of the infidels. Strike off their heads, strike off the very tips of their fingers.
Quran 8:12

DON'T STEAL FROM THE PROPHET

Hadith Book 38, Number 4356:

Narrated Abdullah ibn Umar:
"Some people raided the camels of the Prophet (peace_be_upon_him), drove them off, and apostatised. They killed the herdsman of the Apostle of Allah (peace_be_upon_him) who was a believer. He (the Prophet) sent (people) in pursuit of them and they were caught. He had their hands and feet cut off, and their eyes put out. The verse regarding fighting against Allah and His Prophet (peace_be_upon_him) was then revealed."

Hadith Book Book 019, Number 4363
"The Messenger of Allah (Muhammad-Author) (may peace be upon him) stood up and called out to them (saying): O ye assembly of Jews, accept Islam (and) you will be safe. ....You should know that the earth belongs to Allah and His Apostle (Muhammad-Author), and I wish that I should expel you from this land Those of you who have any property with them should sell it, otherwise they should know that the earth belongs to Allah and His Apostle (and they may have to go away leaving everything behind)."

Hadith Book 019, Number 4366
Book 019, Number 4366:
It has been narrated by 'Umar b. al-Khattib that he heard the Messenger of Allah (Muhammad-author) (may peace be upon him) say: I will expel the Jews and Christians from the Arabian Peninsula and will not leave any but Muslim.

72 VIRGINS

Hadith 2687
The concept of 72 virgins in Islam refers to an aspect of paradise. In a collection by Imam at-Tirmidhi in his "Sunan" (Volume IV, Chapters on "The Features of Heaven as described by the Messenger of Allah", chapter 21: "About the Smallest Reward for the People of Heaven", Hadith 2687) and also quoted by Ibn Kathir in his Tafsir (Qur'anic Commentary) of Surah 55:72, it is stated that:

Abu Sa'id al-Khudhri, who heard the Prophet Muhammad saying, 'The smallest reward for the people of Heaven is an abode where there are eighty thousand servants and seventy two houri (full breasted virgins-Author), over which stands a dome decorated with pearls, aquamarine and ruby, as wide as the distance from al-Jabiyyah to San'a

CHILD MARRIAGE IN ISLAM:

From
http://wiki.answers.com/Q/Did_Muhammed_marry_a_6_year_old_girl
Muhammad married a 9 year old girl. Some say she was 6.

Child marriage is still practiced today.
From
http://www.irishoriginsofcivilization.com/irishoriginsexcerpts/oldpage-irishorigins1.html

CHILD BRIDE DIES AFTER SEX ORGANS RUPTURE FOX NEWS

April 8, 2010

A 13-year-old Yemeni girl who was forced into marriage died five days after her wedding when she suffered a rupture in her sex organs and hemorrhaging, a local rights organization said Thursday.

Ilham Mahdi al Assi died last Friday in a hospital in Yemen's Hajja province, the Shaqaeq Arab Forum for Human Rights said in a statement quoting a medical report.

She was wedded the previous Monday in a traditional arrangement known as a "swap marriage," in which the brother of the bride also married the sister of the groom, it said.

"The child Ilham has died as a martyr due to the abuse of children's lives in Yemen," the non-governmental organization said.

Her death was a " example" of the results of opposing the ban on child marriage in Yemen, which was leading to "killing child females," it said.

The marriage of young girls is widespread in Yemen, which has a strong tribal structure.

a 12-year-old girl in childbirth in September illustrated the case of the country's "brides of death," many of whom were married off even before puberty.

Controversy heightened in Yemen recently over a law banning child marriage in the impoverished country through setting a minimum age of 17 for women and 18 for men.

Thousands of conservative women demonstrated outside parliament last month, answering a call by Islamist parties opposing the law.

A lesser number of women rallied at the same venue a few days later in support of the law, the implementation of which was blocked pending a request by a group of politicians for a review.

MUSLIM CLERICS CAUSE DEATH OF ANOTHER CHILD BRIDE

12-year old Yemeni girl dies three days after wedding Some report she was 13 years old. Who really cares? The fact is that all over Yemen girls die because they are forced to marry too young. This one died because acute bleeding caused by sexual intercourse. A few months ago another died in child birth. A ten year old had to seek a divorce after being raped and beaten. These cases are but a tip of a huge iceberg and they are NOT limited to Yemen. The girls are known as "brides  of death." And no, poverty and tribal customs are not solely to blame. Islamist Imams are, as they fight any legislative effort to ban child marriage. Maktoob News reports Top Yemeni and Saudi clerics fight child marriage ban.

http://www.nytimes.com/2010/05/31/world/asia/31flogging.html?partner=rss&emc=rss

Afghan children are often forced into marriage to older men, and if they escape and are found they are publically flogged, for example with 40 hard lashes and sent back to their families.

"Forced marriage of Afghan girls is not limited to remote rural areas. In Herat city, a Unicef-financed women's shelter run by an Afghan group, the Voice of Women Organization, shelters as many as 60 girls who have fled child marriages.'

Robert Spencer writes:
"Now where did Hamas get the idea that prepubescent girls were of marriageable age? Could it be from Muhammad, the prophet of Islam, the "excellent example" of conduct (cf. Qur'an 33:21)? "The Prophet wrote the (marriage contract) with 'Aisha while she was six years old and consummated his marriage with her while she was nine years old and she remained with him for nine years (i.e. till his death)." (Bukhari 7.62.88)"

SATURDAY, MARCH 13, 2010

Muslim child brides on rise
By TOM GODFREY, Toronto Sun
Last Updated: March 11, 2010 10:46pm

Federal immigration officials say there's little they can do to stop "child brides" from being sponsored into Canada by much older husbands who wed them in arranged marriages abroad.

Top immigration officials in Canada and Pakistan say all they can do is reject the sponsorships of husbands trying to bring their child-brides to Canada. The men have to reapply when the bride turns 16. The marriages are permitted under Sharia Law.

Muslim men, who are Canadian citizens or permanent residents return to their homeland to wed a "child bride" in an arranged marriage in which a dowry is given to the girl's parents. Officials said some of the brides can be 14 years old or younger and are "forced" to marry. The practice occurs in a host of countries including: Afghanistan, Iran, Pakistan and Lebanon.

Not valid in Canada

THE ORIGINS OF ISLAM

From: http://www.truthbeknown.com/islam.htm
by D.M. Murdock/Acharya S

While some may claim that this subjugation and enslavement of women is a cultural tradition, rather than a religious one, it matters not, for it comes hand-in-hand with religions which teach that there is some separate outerspace god who is exclusively male. In Islam, this god is interpreted through the minds of Muslims as being an Arab or Persian man, as opposed to the Jewish man of the Judeo-Christian ideology. This racist, ethnocentric, culturally bigoted and sexist interpretation of any "infinite" god would appear to be absolute nonsense. Yet, in what seems to be supreme arrogance and megalomania, many individuals would like the entire world to believe it is true.

ALLAH—REMAKE OF THE MOON GODDESS

This description of Abraham's origins means that Judaism is built upon hoary myths, such that neither of its offshoot religions, Christianity and Islam, can truthfully claim to be of divine or "inspired" origin. As concerns the god of Islam, Allah, Walker (22) has this to say:

"Late Islamic masculinization of the Arabian Goddess, Al-Lat or Al-Ilat—the Allatu of the Babylonians—formerly worshipped at the Kaaba in Mecca. It has been shown that 'the Allah of Islam' was a male transformation of 'the primitive lunar deity of Arabia.' Her ancient symbol the crescent moon still appears on Islamic flags, even though modern Moslems no longer admit any feminine symbolism whatever connected with the wholly patriarchal Allah."

ASTROTHEOLOGY AT MECCA

One of the sites for this Arab worship of the "hosts of heaven" was Mecca. Regarding the Kaaba of Mecca, that holiest of Muslim holies, Walker (487) writes:

"Shrine of the sacred stone in Mecca, formerly dedicated to the pre-Islamic Triple Goddess Manat, Al-Lat (Allah), and Al-Uzza, the 'Old Woman' worshipped by Mohammed's tribesmen the Koreshites. The stone was also called Kubaba, Kuba or Kube, and has been linked with the name of Cybele (Kybela), the Great Mother of the Gods. The stone bore the emblem of the yoni , like the Black Stone worshipped by votaries of Artemis. Now it is regarded as the holy center of patriarchal Islam, and its feminine symbolism has been lost, though priests of the Kaaba are still known as Sons of the Old Woman."

And a translator of the Koran, N.J. Dawood (1), says:

"Long before Muhammad's call, Arabian paganism was showing signs of decay. At the Ka'bah the Meccans worshipped not only Allah, the supreme Semitic God, but also a number of female deities whom they regarded as daughters of Allah. Among these were Al-Lat, Al-Uzza and Manat, who represented the Sun, Venus and Fortune respectively."

ARABIAN MATRIARCHY

Concerning the nation of Arabia, Walker asserts that, prior to the encroachment of Islam, it was a matriarchal culture for over 1,000 years.

"The Annals of Ashurbanipal said Arabia was governed by queens for as long as anyone could remember....

"Mohammed's legends clearly gave him a matriarchal family background. His parents' marriage was matrilocal. His mother remained with her own family and received her husband as an occasional visitor....

"Pre-Islamic Arabia was dominated by the female-centered clans. Marriages were matrilocal, inheritance matrilineal. Polyandry—several husbands to one wife—was common. Men lived in their wives' homes. Divorce was initiated by the wife. If she turned her tent to face east for three nights in a row, the husband was dismissed and forbidden to enter the tent again.

"Doctrines attributed to Mohammed simply re-versed the ancient system in favor of men. A Moslem husband could dismiss his wife by saying 'I divorce thee' three times. As in Europe, the change from matriarchate to patriarchate came about only gradually and with much strife.

 "With or without Mohammed, Islam succeeded in becoming completely male-dominated, making no place for women except in slavery or in the seclusion of the harem. Islamic mosques still bear signs reading: 'Women and dogs and other impure animals are not permitted to enter.'

"Nevertheless, traces of the Goddess proved ineradicable. Like the virgin Mary, Arabia's Queen of Heaven received a mortal form and a subordinate position as Fatima, Mohammed's 'daughter.' But she was no real daughter. She was known as Mother of her Father, and Source of the Sun..."

WHO WROTE THE KORAN?

As concerns the Koran, the Muslim holy book, Walker (513) says:

"Mohammedan scriptures, often erroneously thought to have been written by Mohammed. Moslems don't believe this. But many don't know the Koran was an enlarged revised version of the ancient Word of the Goddess Kore, revered by Mohammed's tribe, the Koreshites (Children of Kore), who guarded her shrine at Mecca.

"The original writing was done long before Mohammed's time by holy imams, a word related to Semitic ima, 'mother.' Like the original mahatmas or 'great mothers' of India, the original imams were probably priestesses of the old Arabian matriarchate. It was said they took the scripture from a prototype that existed in heaven from the beginning of eternity, 'Mother of the Book'—i.e., the Goddess herself, wearing the Book of Fate on her breast as Mother Tiamat wore the Tablets of Destiny. Sometimes the celestial Koran was called the Preserved Tablet. There was some resemblance between this and other legendary books of divine origin, such as the Ur-text, the Book of Thoth, and the Emerald Tablet of Hermes.

"As in the case of the Judeo-Christian Bible, the Koran was much rewritten to support new patriarchal laws and to obliterate the figures of the Goddess and her priestesses."

In The Great Religious Leaders, Charles Frances Potter says of Mohammed, "It is very doubtful that he read any of the Bible: indeed, it has not been proved that he ever read anything, or wrote anything. He called himself 'the illiterate prophet.'" Of course, much of the Koran is based on the Bible, both Old and

New Testaments, combined with pre-Islamic Arab and other traditions.

Regarding the unoriginality of the Koran, Islam expert Dr. Daniel Pipes says (The Jerusalem Post, 5/12/00):

"The Koran is a not a product of Muhammad or even of Arabia, but a collection of earlier Judeo-Christian liturgical materials stitched together to meet the needs of a later age."

Biblical scholar Dr. Robert M. Price likewise concurs as to the pre-Islamic nature of various koranic texts:

"The Koran was assembled from a variety of prior Hagarene texts (hence the contradictions re Jesus' death) in order to provide the Moses-like Muhammad with a Torah of his own...."

Islamic expert Dr. Gerd-R. Puin concludes:

"My idea is that the Koran is a kind of cocktail of texts that were not all understood even at the time of Muhammad. Many of them may even be a hundred years older than Islam itself. Even within Islamic traditions there is a huge body of contradictory information, including a significant Christian substrate...."

Thus, the Koran was not written by Mohammed.

Acharya concludes (this URL): "If this world is to survive into the coming age, we will need as many people as possible to drop all of these divisive doctrines. What we need on this planet, right now, are honest, caring and whole human beings who are motivated not by potential favors and rewards from sadistic and ethnocentric deities in the sky but by innate decency and integrity. Only in this way can we all live in peace rather than fear, which is the weapon wielded by religion to convert the "faithful."

WHY I BECAME A SKEPTIC

Probably the best class that I took at the University of California at Berkeley was a speech class from Professor Telfer. It turned out to be much more than about speechmaking.

In one of the first classes, he pointed to someone in the class, almost at random it seemed – "What religion are you?" Even today, one doesn't pry that sharply into the internal beliefs of anyone. You don't touch the subject of religion or politics (politics was next!) in polite society, out of the blue, like that. A student answered "Catholic", or was it "Protestant", I don't remember right now, but it was one. Let's assume the student said "Catholic".

"Why are you a Catholic?" Telfer asked. "Are your parents Catholic?" The student said "Yes". "Have you investigated any other religion? , he pursued further. "No" was the answer. "Don't you think you should?" My, this class was about questioning your own beliefs, not just about speechmaking. Plus being skeptical why you hold certain beliefs.

This was going to be an interesting class!

Of course he asked another student, who turned out to be Protestant. "Are your parents Protestant?" "Yes". "Have you investigated any other religion?" Then to another student, again randomly, it appeared, "What political party do you favor?" The student answered, say, "Republican". "Have you investigated the other political parties?" As if that would be the natural thing for you to have done, before you accepted your parent's political (or religious) beliefs wholesale without question, just because they were the ones they followed.

After that class, whenever someone made a statement, in my mind I felt that I could question whether it was true or not, almost automatically, in my mind, at least. And maybe do further research on the statement. How many times has it been that someone sends an email to me, and obviously to a bunch of recipients, that I have checked it out on "Snopes" or done further research on the truth of the statement, and found it wasn't true? I can't count.

Professor Telfer's class was not just about speechmaking. It was also about **critical thinking**.

That year at Cal was the happiest year of my young life. I felt "FREE"! and happy to have become a skeptical free thinker, enriching my later conscious life. My appreciation and gratitude go out to Professor Telfer for that upgrade to my life.

MORMONISM AND VIOLENCE

Violence perpetrated by Mormons- "The militiamen (Mormons organized to fight the U.S. Army-Author) and their tribesmen auxiliaries executed approximately 120 men, women and children." These unfortunates were emigrants from Arkansas going to California.

"If any miserable scoundrels come here, cut their throats." Brigham Young.

"The Mountain Meadows Massacre stands without a parallel amongst the crimes that stain the pages of American history. It was a crime committed without cause or justification of any kind to relieve it of its fearful character... When nearly exhausted from fatigue and thirst, [the men of the caravan] were approached by white men, with a flag of truce, and induced to surrender their arms, under the most solemn promises of protection. They were then murdered in cold blood." William Bishop, Attorney to John D. Lee.

http://www.religioustolerance.org/lds_mass.htm   also

September 1857. The Mountain Meadows Massacre http://en.wikipedia.org/wiki/Mountain_Meadows_massacre

 Most know about Mormon cannabalism of their own people (for survival purposes –
http://en.wikipedia.org/wiki/Donner_party) 1846-1847.

Originally and for decades, Mormonism included polygamy (Ok for men, but not for women).

In the beginning, Scholars generally count about 30 wives for Smith. http://en.wikipedia.org/wiki/Plural_marriage

Mormons believed in "Blood Vengeance" (-justified killing- no turning the other cheek)

MORMONISM HISTORY IS RIFE WITH VIOLENCE

http://www.exmormon.org/violence.htm
Joseph Smith, founder of the Mormon faith, finds gold plates that nobody can see under the pain of instant death, and verbally translates them into the Book of Mormon to scribes who also cannot look at them. The plates eventually ascended to heaven forever. (Author)

JOSEPH SMITH AND THE GOLD PLATES

http://hismin.com/?q=content/joseph-smith-and-gold-plates

"Imagine Joseph Smith wrapping his linen shirt around this 200 pound block of gold plates, tucking it casually under his arm and strolling off towards home, some three miles distance! Imagine him further, running at the top of his speed through the woods, jumping over logs, and knocking down not one or two, but three assailants in the process, all the while with the 200 pounds of gold plates safely under his arm! If anyone would care to experiment, lead is the nearest common metal to gold in weight, its specific gravity being 11.35. Try tucking a 200 pound block of lead under your arm, and running and leaping through the woods with it for three miles! Then ask yourself: Can I believe Joseph Smith's Story? "

http://hismin.com/?q=content/joseph-smith-and-gold-plates

Joseph Smith, the prophet and founder of the Church of Jesus Christ of Latter-day Saints (Mormons) tells us that the Book of Mormon was translated from some golden plates shown to him by a heavenly messenger on September 21, 1823.

"While I was thus in the act of calling upon God I discovered a light appearing in the room which continued to increase until the room was lighter than at noonday, when immediately a personage appeared at my bedside standing in the air for his feet did not touch the floor...When I first looked upon him I was afraid, but the fear soon left me. He called me by name, and said unto me that he was a messenger sent from the presence of God to me, and that his name was Nephi. [9] That God had a work for me to do, and that my name should be had for good and evil, among all nations, kindreds, and tongues; or that it should be both good and evil spoken of among all people. He said there was a book deposited written upon **gold plates**, giving an account of the former inhabitants of this continent, and the source from whence they sprang. He also said that the fullness of the everlasting gospel was contained in it, [10] as delivered by the Savior to the ancient inhabitants. Also that there were two stones in silver bows, and these stones fastened to a breastplate constituted what is called the Urim and Thummim, deposited with the plates, and the possession and use of these stones was what constituted seers in ancient or former times, and that God had prepared them for the purpose of translating the book." (Times and Seasons, vol. 3, p. 753; Comp.with Pearl of Great Price, p.52)

THE PLATES ARE SHOWN TO JOSEPH

"Convenient to the village of Manchester, Ontario Co. New York, stands a hill of considerable size, and the most elevated on any in the neighbor hood (sic Author); on the west side of this hill not far from the top, under a stone on (sic Author) considerable size, lay the plates deposited in a stone box: this stone was thick and rounding in the middle on the upper side, and thinner towards the edges, so that the middle part of it was visible above the ground, but the edge all round was covered with earth. Having removed the earth and obtained a lever which I got fixed under the edge of the stone and with a little exertion raised it up, I looked in and there indeed I beheld the plates, the Urim and Thummim and the Breastplate as stated by the messenger. The box in which they lay was formed by laying stones together in some kind of cement; in the bottom of the box were laid two stones crossways of the box, and on these stones lay the plates and the other things with them. I made an attempt to take them out but was forbidden by the messenger and was again informed that the time for bringing them forth had not yet arrived, neither would until four years from that time." (Times and Seasons, vol. 3, p. 771; Comp. with Pearl of Great Price, p. 54-55)

THE PLATES DESCRIBED

In a letter to John Wentworth, editor of the Chicago Democrat, Joseph Smith described the plates in some detail:

"These records were engraven on plates which had the appearance of gold, **each plate was six inches wide and eight inches long and not quite so thick as common tin.** They were filled with engraving, in Egyptian characters and bound together in a volume, as the leaves of a book with three rings running through the whole. **The volume was something near six inches in thickness,** a part of which was sealed. The characters on the unsealed part were small, and beautifully engraved. The whole book exhibited many marks of antiquity in its construction and much skill in the art of engraving." (Times and Seasons, vol. 3, p. 707, March 1, 1842; Comp. with History of the Church, vol. 4, p. 537)

JOSEPH RECEIVES THE GOLDEN PLATES

"At length the time arrived for obtaining the plates, and Urim and Thummim, and the breastplate; on the 22nd day of

98

September, 1827, having went as usual at the end of another year to the place where they were deposited, the same heavenly messenger delivered them up to me, with this charge that I should be responsible for them: that if I should let them go carelessly or through any neglect of mine I should be cut off; but that if I would use all my endeavors to preserve them, until he the messenger should call for them, they should be protected...by the wisdom of God they remained safe in my hands until I had accomplished by them what was required at my hands when according to arrangements the messenger called for them, I delivered them up to him and he has them in his charge until this day." (Times and Seasons, vol. 3, p. 772; Comp. with Pearl of Great Price, p. 55-56)

JOSEPH SAVES THE PLATES FROM THREE ASSAILANTS

After removing the plates from the stone box, Joseph hid them in a birch log until preparations could be made at home for the plates. then he went to retrieve them.

"The plates were secreted about three miles from home...Joseph, on coming to them, took them from their secret place, and wrapping them in his linen frock, placed them under his arm and started for home."

After proceeding a short distance, he thought it would be more safe to leave the road and go through the woods. Traveling some distance after he left the road, he came to a large windfall (sic Author), and as he was **jumping over a log,** a man sprang up from behind it, and gave him a heavy blow with a gun. Joseph turned around and knocked him down, then ran at the top of his speed. About half a mile further he was attacked again in the same manner as before; he knocked this man down in like manner as the former, and ran on again; and before he reached home he was assaulted the third time. In striking the last one he dislocated his thumb, which, however, he did not notice until he came within sight of the house, when he threw himself down in the corner of the fence in order to recover his breath. As soon as he was able, he arose and came to the house." (Lucy Mack Smith, mother of Joseph Smith, in Biographical Sketches of Joseph Smith the Prophet, 1853, pp. 104-105; Comp. reprinted edition by Bookcraft Publishers in 1956 under the title History of Joseph Smith by His Mother, pp. 107- 108) Emphasis added.

THE WEIGHT OF THE PLATES

The weight of the plates makes the story incredible. The heavenly messenger told Joseph Smith that plates were of gold. Joseph described the plates as being 6 inches wide, 8 inches long, and something near 6 inches in thickness. Gold has certain interesting properties. It is a **very heavy metal,** its specific gravity being 19.3. It is very soft and malleable. Plates made of gold would therefore pack down very tightly when stacked. A little figuring will reveal to the reader that **the plates weighed 200.81 pounds or thereabouts!**

The base of the monument on the hill in New York where Joseph Smith allegedly found the golden plates depicts him kneeling and receiving the 200 pound plates from the heavenly messenger with outstretched arms. Quite a physical feat!

Imagine Joseph Smith wrapping his linen shirt around this 200 pound block of gold plates, tucking it casually under his arm and strolling off towards home, some three miles distance! Imagine him further, running at the top of his speed through the woods, jumping over logs, and knocking down not one or two, but three assailants in the process, all the while with the 200 pounds of gold plates safely under his arm! If anyone would care to experiment, lead is the nearest common metal to gold in weight, its specific gravity being 11.35. Try tucking a 200 pound block of lead under your arm, and running and leaping through the woods with it for three miles! Then ask yourself: Can I believe Joseph Smith's Story?

Joseph Smith made the ludicrous mistake because he was dealing with imaginary gold. While real gold is very heavy, imaginary gold weighs nothing at all. And that is what Joseph Smith's golden plates were -- imaginary.

1 - In later versions of this account the heavenly messenger's name is changed to Moroni.

2 – There is a list of "everlasting" doctrines that are not contained in the Book of Mormon.

OFFSHOOT OF CHURCH OF LATTER DAY SAINTS GONE ASTRAY

http://en.wikipedia.org/wiki/Warren_Jeffs
(Sex crime allegations and FBI's Most Wanted List)

In part:
"Warren Steed Jeffs (born December 3, 1955 in San Francisco, California) was the president of the Fundamentalist Church of Jesus Christ of Latter Day Saints (FLDS Church) from 2002 to 2007. He may still be the Prophet of the FLDS Church, as no certain statements have been made that he stepped aside from this position after his conviction in 2007. While president and "Prophet, Seer and Revelator" of the organization, Jeffs wielded considerable religious as well as secular power, in line with the FLDS Church's theocratic principles. While president and "Prophet, Seer and Revelator" of the organization, Jeffs wielded considerable religious as well as secular power, in line with the FLDS Church's theocratic principles."

"In January 2004, Jeffs expelled a group of 20 men from Colorado City, including the mayor, and reassigned their wives and children to other men in the community. Jeffs, like his predecessors, continued the standard FLDS and Mormon fundamentalist tenet that faithful men must follow what is known as the doctrine of "Celestial Marriage" or plural marriage in order to attain the highest degree of Exaltation in the afterlife. Jeffs specifically taught that a devoted church member is expected to have at least three wives in order to get into heaven, and the more wives a man has, the closer he is to heaven. Former church members claim that Jeffs himself has seventy wives (Egan, 2005)."

"Jeffs, the sole individual in the church who possessed the authority to perform its marriages, was responsible for assigning wives to husbands. Jeffs also held the authority to discipline wayward male believers by "reassigning their wives, children and homes to another man."

FOUNDER OF MORMONISM

Before founding Mormonism, Founder of Mormonism Joseph Smith was convicted on March 20, 1826 of being an imposter: http://mormonconspiracy.com/book-of-mormon.html
Reading the case, one concludes that today we would say he was convicted of fraud.

Joseph Smith, the founder of the Mormon movement, had at least 24 wives. One was 14 years old, and after the marriage considered herself as an abused child. Here is a list of his wives from official church records:

http://www.familysearch.org/Eng/Search/AF/individual_record
.asp?recid=7762167&lds=0

Brigham Young was the President of The Church of Jesus Christ of Latter-day Saints (LDS Church "Mormon" Church) from 1847 for 30 years, until his death.

Young had 55 wives. One was 15 years old. Young had 57 children by 16 of his wives. Here is a list of his 55 wives:

http://en.wikipedia.org/wiki/List_of_Brigham_Young's_wives

BUDDHA

He (Gautama Siddhartha) is reported to have born in 540 B.C. according to some sources, in 563 in others, in 624, or 642, or 644 in others. See http://www.sacredsites.com/asia/india/buddhist.html

He became enlightened under the Bodhi tree.

There were 3 Buddhas before him. They also went to Bodh Gaya and became enlightened there.

From the above: "Preeminent among all these pilgrimage sites, both old and new, is Bodh Gaya, the place where the Buddha attained enlightenment. As mentioned earlier, this site is traditionally believed to be the place where the Buddhas of the three previous ages had also attained enlightenment."

Buddha never wrote anything down (Neither did Jesus or Mohammad-Author). His philosophy was reported by reported disciples. No archaeological remains have been found of any structures dating from the time of the historical Buddha; the earliest temple seems to have been constructed by the Emperor Asoka around 250 BC. (This is at least 290 years after his reported latest birth, and 394 years after other estimates of his birth.-Author)

Three months after the Paranirvana (passing-Author), five hundred of his chief disciples met in a cave at Rajagraha (must have been a big cave-Author) and by common consensus agreed upon what were to be considered the main teachings of the Buddha. Considerable disagreement arose among them on the finer points of the Buddha's message as is evident from the fact that by the year 100 BC eighteen separate sects had been formed, each with its own interpretation.

Buddha's birth. Buddha's mother, Queen Maya, was a virgin who, in a dream was visited by a white elephant (considered sacred and heralded as a manifestation of the Gods) who impregnated virgin Maya, by piercing her side painlessly with one of his six tusks, who in turn brought Buddha into flesh.

(do a search on elephant, Maya, and Buddha)

Example, from Encyclopedia Britannica:

http://www.britannica.com/eb/topic-357776/Maha-Maya

.....''his mother, the queen Maha Maya, dreamed that a white elephant had entered her womb. Ten lunar months later, as she strolled in the garden of Lumbini, the child emerged from under her right arm. He was able to walk and talk immediately.''

Buddhism in its teaching, but not necessarily in practice, is one of the most peaceful religions (some say it is not a religion at all-it is a philosophy) of them all. Being a suspicious person about the connection between religion and violence, I was looking for but could not at first find any violence sanctioned or encouraged in any of the so called Buddha's teachings. On the contrary, from the World Council of Churches:

From: http://www.wcc-coe.org/wcc/what/interreligious/cd39-03.html

"Buddhist teachings maintain that under any circumstance, whether it is political, religious, cultural or ethnic, violence cannot be accepted or advocated in solving disputes between nations. All Buddhist traditions unanimously agree that war cannot be the solution to disputes and conflicts either. Even for achieving a religious goal, violence cannot be used and justified. A Buddhist cannot imagine a principle of 'Just War.' How can a 'war' become a 'just' one? How can the slaughter of human beings be justified as 'morally right'?   P.D. Premasiri has convincingly asserted by examining early Buddhist standpoint that even in the case of solving social conflicts such as war, Buddhism "does not advocate violence under any circumstance." [11] When 'insider' perspectives are examined across Buddhist cultures and combined with doctrinal understandings, one can create a context in comprehending Buddhist abhorrence for violence and encouragement in seeking creative strategies for a non-violent path in overcoming violence."

SOME BUDDHISTS ARE VIOLENT

BUDDHIST NATIONALISM AND RELIGIOUS VIOLENCE IN SRI LANKA

Introduction
Recently the Śri Lankān people have witnessed more religious violence than ever before. It has spread from the conflict with the Tamil Tigers to Buddhist attacks on Muslims and Christians, and now counter attacks by aggrieved Muslims. .....

While the world community has rightly condemned the LTTE (Liberation Tigers of Tamil Eelam) and its brutal acts, fewer people are cognizant of the role that militant Buddhists have played in this conflict. Here, for example, are excerpts of songs published by the government, of the Buddhist monk Elle Gunavamsa:

> The sword is pulled from the [scabbard], it is
> Not put back unless smeared with blood.
> I turned by blood to milk to make you grow
> Not for myself but for the country
> My brave, brilliant soldier son
> Leaving [home] to defend the motherland
> That act of merit is enough
> To reach Nirvāna in a future birth.[3]

Many in the world community would be shocked to learn that these lines were composed by a Buddhist monk.

During 2003-04, 165 Śri Lankān Christian churches were attacked by Buddhist mobs, resulting in the complete destruction of some, the stoning of parsonages, the smashing of statues, and the burning (of) Bibles and hymnals. Śri Lankā has the largest percentage of Christians in South Asia, and 25 percent of those are Tamils. (The father of Tamil nationalism was a Malaysian Christian by the name of J. V. Chelvanayakam.) Christians say that one reason they are being targeted is that they are accused of being Tamil sympathizers. The other reason is that Protestant Christian missionaries have had considerable success in recent years, which has led to Buddhist charges of unethical conversions. One website claims that Evangelicals and Pentecostals have increased from 50,000 to 240,000 since 1980. The missionaries can also claim that they are simply making up for lost ground because before the rise of neo-Buddhism in the late 19th Century there were many more Christians on the island.

But wait, there's more, in Tibet, for example:

From:
http://www.dissidentvoice.org/Articles9/Parenti_Tibet.htm

Sample:
The poor and afflicted were taught that they had brought their troubles upon themselves because of their foolish and wicked ways in previous lives. Hence they had to accept the misery of their present existence as an atonement and in anticipation that their lot would improve upon being reborn. The rich and powerful of course treated their good fortune as a reward for-- and tangible evidence of-virtue in past and present lives.

TORTURE AND MUTILATION IN SHANGHRI-LA

In the Dalai Lama's Tibet, torture and mutilation---including eye gouging, the pulling out of tongues, hamstringing, and amputation of arms and legs--were favored punishments inflicted upon thieves, runaway serfs, and other "criminals." Journeying through Tibet in the 1960s, Stuart and Roma Gelder interviewed a former serf, Tsereh Wang Tuei, who had stolen two sheep belonging to a monastery. For this he had both his eyes gouged out and his hand mutilated beyond use. He explains that he no longer is a Buddhist: "When a holy lama told them to blind me I thought there was no good in religion." [12] Some Western visitors to Old Tibet remarked on the number of amputees to be seen. Since it was against Buddhist teachings to take human life, some offenders were severely lashed and then "left to God" in the freezing night to die. "The parallels between Tibet and medieval Europe are striking," concludes Tom Grunfeld in his book on Tibet. [13]

Some monasteries had their own private prisons, reports Anna Louise Strong. In 1959, she visited an exhibition of torture equipment that had been used by the Tibetan overlords. There were handcuffs of all sizes, including small ones for children, and instruments for cutting off noses and ears, and breaking off hands. For gouging out eyes, there was a special stone cap with two holes in it that was pressed down over the head so that the eyes bulged out through the holes and could be more readily torn out. There were instruments for slicing off kneecaps and heels, or hamstringing legs. There were hot brands, whips, and special implements for disembowling. [14] The exhibition presented photographs and testimonies of victims who had been blinded or crippled or suffered amputations for thievery. There was the shepherd whose master owed him a reimbursement in yuan and wheat but refused to pay. So he took one of the master's cows; for this he had his hands severed. Another herdsman, who opposed having his wife taken from him by his lord, had his hands broken off. There were pictures of Communist activists with noses and upper lips cut off, and a woman who was raped and then had her nose sliced away. [15]

Theocratic despotism had been the rule for generations. An English visitor to Tibet in 1895, Dr. A. L. Waddell, wrote that the Tibetan people were under the "intolerable tyranny of monks" and the devil superstitions they had fashioned to terrorize the people. In 1904 Perceval Landon described the Dalai Lama's rule as "an engine of oppression" and "a barrier to all human improvement." At about that time, another English traveler, Captain W.F.T. O'Connor, observed that "the great landowners and the priests . . . exercise each in their own dominion a despotic power from which there is no appeal," while the people are "oppressed by the most monstrous growth of monasticism and priest-craft the world has ever seen." Tibetan rulers, like those of Europe during the Middle Ages, "forged innumerable weapons of servitude, invented degrading legends and stimulated a spirit of superstition" among the common people. [16]

GENDER IMBALANCE

From Mijares, Sharon G., Rafea A., Falik, R., and Schipper, J.E. (2007) The Root of All Evil: An Exposition of Prejudice, Fundamentalism and Gender Imbalance UK: Imprint Academic, Charlottesville, VA: Imprint Academic. pp 32-34

Gender-imbalance is the most powerful example of the repressive qualities exemplified in patriarchy for it demands that the female be subservient to the male. Men have held the monopoly and authority on administrative and religious matters since patriarchy's onset. In modem times, the Taliban regime portrayed gender imbalance for the entire world to see through the eyes of modem media. Only males were visible, as Afghan women were despised and hidden from view. The Taliban created its own interpretations of Islamic teachings. Its behaviors were predominantly aggressive and destructive as a result of the extreme gender imbalance. The Taliban men evidenced a lack of caring and respect for anything outside of their own rigid ideology (for example, not only their violent treatment of women, but also their destruction of art, including the precious Buddhist statues of antiquity and disallowance of music in any form).

But the Taliban men were not alone in these gender imbalanced attitudes. For example, Catholic and Protestant Christian denominations have followed the command- of the apostle Paul, "Let your women keep silence in the churches: for it is not permitted unto them to speak; but they are commanded to be under obedience, as also saith the [Jewish] law. And if they learn anything, let them ask their husbands at home: for it is a shame for women to speak in the church" (I Corinthians, 14:34-35). And, as noted, this was a Jewish law expecting females to adhere to male dominance so this thread wove itself through Judaism, Christianity and Islam alike.

From the onset of patriarchal dominance, every religion-from East to West-claimed male dominance over " This stance must now change.

THE SPLITTING OF HEAVEN AND EARTH

Gender balance represents a significant element in restoring humanity from the brink of destruction. Women are inherently disposed to egalitarian principles because of their innate maternal and relational qualities. Also, there is significant evidence to verify that gender-balanced, pre-patriarchal societies lived more harmoniously than those under patriarchal rule. The onset of patriarchy began approximately six thousand years ago. Anthropological explorations have revealed that Paleolithic (around 20,000+8000 BCE) and Neolithic (approximately 8000 to 4000 BCE) cultures were primarily egalitarian (Eisler, 1987). Gravesites from that period also suggest egalitarian cultural values. For example, excavations of gravesites revealed that marital partners, children, animals and slaves not buried along with the deceased. (That phenomenon, indicative of values associated with domination (Eisler, 1987), was evidenced in the later gravesites of patriarchal cultures.)

These prehistoric cultures revered the Great Mother. Numerous icons depicting feminine representations of God have been found as anthropologists and archeologists unearthed ancient temples and dwellings. Yet there were no indications that males were subservient to females. Dwelling places and gravesites were not suggestive of vast differences in wealth and status amongst the citizenry. These discoveries have also confirmed that earlier beliefs differed considerably from the later Judeo-Christian story of Adam, the rib and the fall from grace (blamed on Eve and damning the feminine) (Parrinder, 1971; Eliade, 1978). They provided evidence of a very different paradigm, one in which iconography suggests that females were revered because of their capacity to bring forth life (Stone, 1976) and also that earlier societies appeared to live more peacefully.

The shift to patriarchal dominance began to develop around 4000 BCE. Since patriarchy was based upon a strict male lineage, there was a distinct change in social organization and religious beliefs. Patriarchal ideology, by its very nature, required a masculine representation and definition of God. New creation stories were formed from the old ones. Jack Miles, author of the Pulitzer Prize winning book God: A Biography, notes how "Myth, legend, and history mix endlessly in the Bible," and "that Bible historians are endlessly sorting them out" (Miles, 1995, p. 13). But one thing that is consistent is that the Bible has been interpreted from a one-sided patriarchal perspective.

REPEAT

THE TEN PRINCIPLES FOR A GLOBAL RATIONAL HUMANISM
THE CODE FOR GLOBAL ETHICS
1. DIGNITY: Proclaim the natural dignity and inherent worth of all human beings.
2. RESPECT: Respect the life and property of others.
3. TOLERANCE: Be tolerant of others' beliefs and lifestyles.
4. SHARING: Share with those who are less fortunate and assist those who are in need of help.
5. NO DOMINATION: Do not dominate through lies or otherwise.
6. NO SUPERSTITION: Rely on reason, logic, and science to understand the Universe and to solve life's problems.
7. CONSERVATION: Conserve and improve the Earth's natural environment.
8. NO WAR: Resolve differences and conflicts without resorting to war or violence.
9. DEMOCRACY: Rely on political and economic democracy to organize human affairs.

10. EDUCATION: Develop one's intelligence and talents through education and effort.

From "The Code for Global Ethics, Ten Humanist Principles" by Rodrigue Tremblay, with Preface by Paul Kurtz. Published 2010 by Prometheus Books.

EPILOGUE

What Mysteries Lie BEYOND RELIGION?

An unbelievable happening can lead you to be open to other beliefs that you normally wouldn't consider believable. An unbelievable event happened to me in a conference many years ago in Marin County. A minister told us a story that, unbeknownst to his parishioners, he was under heavy sedation at San Rafael General Hospital on a Saturday night.

Later in the next week, a couple from Fairfax told him "That was a great conversation we had last Saturday night". The minister told the couple that that was impossible, and that unbeknownst to them he was under sedation at San Rafael General Hospital.

They said no, that couldn't be. You talked to us for two hours. It was a great conversation, they insisted. Not only that, another couple about 30 miles north in Novato told the minister "That was a great conversation we had Saturday night." They also mentioned he had talked to them for about 2 hours.

Go figure: I believe the minister. But that means that he teleported to two different places SIMULTANEOUSLY. Also it means that time is mysterious. Can we say he time-traveled here?

Now it gets worse. At the same conference a guy said that he flipped his motorcycle, in front of a Mack truck and the Mack truck's tire was headed straight toward his head. He said that his whole life went before him.

Kind of skeptically, I guess, I said, "That's interesting. Was it in Technicolor?" He said "Yes" I said, "Tell me, was it from when you were a baby, up to that present moment?(on the pavement) or was it from that present moment to when you were a baby?" He said, "It was from the present moment backward to when I was a baby". I said "Everything?" He said "Everything."

Go figure. If true, and I have no reason to think he was making this up, there is something weird about time. It couldn't have been more than fractions of a second or a second before the tire swerved and just missed him. So time can be compressed so that a lot of consciousness can fit into a short period of time. Others in accidents tell about time slowing down and things go into slow motion.

In Autobiography of a Yogi, Paramahansa Yogananda tells in Chapter 3 ("The Saint with Two Bodies") about meeting in Banaras, when he was 12 years old, with Kedar Nath Babu, a person Paramahansa was supposed to contact on a business matter on behalf of his father. His father told Paramahansa that another friend of his father, Swami Pranabananda, would help him get in touch with Kedar Nath Babu. Paramahansa was at the residence of the Swami, when Kedar Nath Bagu appeared at the door of the Swami. He had been at the Ganges bathing when the Swami approached Kedar Nath Babu and told him of Paramahansa's presence at the Swami's residence.

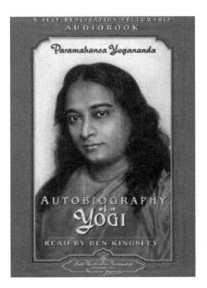

This happened while Paramahansa in the Swami's residence, and while the Swami didn't leave Paramahansa's sight! Swami Pranabananda said to Paramahansa "Why are you so stupefied at all this? The subtle unity of the phenomenal world is not hidden from true yogis. I instantly see and converse with my disciples in distant Calcutta. They can similarly transcend at will every obstacle of gross matter."

There are other examples of what I would call teleportation in **Autobiography of a Yogi.**

Shirley Maclaine and Film Materializations
http://sathyasaibabaji.blogspot.com/2005/07/shirley-maclaine-and-film.html

Shirley Maclaine, film star, spiritual teacher, political activist, was a guest on the Larry King Show. She told his audience that her friend Richard Bock had gone to India to film Sai Baba. This is very difficult since Baba discourages publicity. Bock ran out of a color film while in India.. a film which could only be purchased in California. Baba excused himself from the room a moment... and came back with a film store bag which said Beverly Hills Camera Shop. A receipt was stapled to it. Inside was color film.

After he returned to California, Bock went to the shop where a clerk told him that on the day in question a man in an orange robe and Afro had come in to purchase the film, and had not waited for change.

I heard another story about a ring that Sai Baba gave to someone and it had Tiffany's inscribed inside it. When the person got to New York, he went into Tiffany's and asked

Sai Baba 1927-2011

who bought this ring, and they said "you wouldn't believe who bought this ring!".... and described a man in an orange robe and Afro.

We have a personal friend, Suzanne, who went to Sai Baba's ashram and witnessed physical manifestations.

My wife Karen lived in India seven years as a student with a classical art major, met Mother Teresa twice, and was about to marry a young Indian man, but was somewhat worried about his dominant mother. She woke up from a dream where Sai Baba appeared in white silk robe and she could feel the pressure of his hand on her left shoulder. Actually for some time later during that day she continued to feel the pressure of his hand. She took that as a message that she shouldn't marry the young man, mainly because of the potential mother-in-law. THANK you, Sai Baba!

A TURNING POINT: An Insane Night in the Basement of Children's Hospital in San Francisco. I was a logical "show-me-the-evidence" analytic type person in 1970. After all, at University at Berkeley, my major was economics with a minor in mathematics. BORING. No spirituality or thinking outside the box there.

In that basement of Children's Hospital in San Francisco **everything** changed. At that time I was a commercial real estate broker, working as a Vice President for United States Real Estate Corporation which had offices in the Bank of America World Headquarters in San Francisco. I had an offer on some commercially zoned land across from the Lake Tahoe Airport owned by a doctor in Palo Alto, 45 miles away.

I called the doctor and said "I have an offer on your land and I wanted to come down to Palo Alto and present the offer to you." He said "You don't have to drive down because I am coming up tonight to a meeting in the basement of Children's Hospital in San Francisco and you can present it to me there.

Like a good broker, I showed up 15 minutes early and sat in a chair outside the large room where the meeting was to be held. People in white uniforms were showing up and I noticed an air of excitement. A nurse came up to me and excitingly asked me "are you Alexander Everett?" I said no, and wondered who the heck Alexander Everett was.

The doctor from Palo Alto was late, so I sat in the back of the room filled with doctors and nurses in front. Alexander, a very impressive man, explained the power of the alpha level of brain frequency, and said that by making your brain go to the alpha level, which I recall was 7 to 11 cycles per second, you can do amazing things.

As a demonstration, Alexander had a 17 year old boy with no medical training diagnose patients known to members of the audience. The only information the kid was given was the patient's age, name and location. Then this 17 year old kid from Laredo, Texas would close his eyes and go to the alpha level and "scan" the body of the patient, and would use medical terms giving his diagnosis.

After each diagnosis, Alexander would ask the doctor or nurse if that was accurate, and invariably the answer was "yes, that is correct". There were many diagnoses and the answer was always that the diagnosis was correct. Amazingly, one doctor asked the 17 year old if the patient was going to live or die from the particular problem, because the patient was the doctor's mother! (she was in Switzerland, I recall)

I thought to myself that this was the weirdest thing that I had ever seen.

I did present the offer to the doctor who came up from Palo Alto, 45 miles away, and the next day when I went back to work in the Bank of America building I told one of the girls there about this amazing demonstration by Alexander Everett, who had learned this technique from Dr. José Silva in Laredo, Texas.

Alexander Everett, Author– "The Genius Within You (1921–2005)

A couple of weeks later, the girl told me "you know the guy you told me about, Alexander Everett? He is coming to San Francisco and is going to give training on the alpha technique. Of course, I signed up when he started the training, which was called "Mind Dynamics". I learned the technique to get your mind to the alpha level, using the colors of the rainbow, and numbers declining from 7 to 1.

At the end of the training there was a graduation exercise where you were supposed to diagnose a person at a distance. I sat across from a lady who gave me a name, age and location of an individual who was 8000 miles away in the Philippines. I closed my eyes and scanned the body, and I said, "I can't see anything on his right arm beyond about the elbow." I heard a gasp from the lady sitting opposite. She said "I was seeing if you could catch the minor ear operation he had recently." She then told me that he had a withered right arm since he was a child, and it was so natural to her, that she didn't even think of that.

Alexander was a teacher of teachers, and is known at the father of the human potential movement. He had instructors who went on to teach others. One was Stuart Emory, from Australia, who taught "Actualizations", which I took later. Another was John Hanley, who started "Lifespring" and I took both the basic and the advanced courses.

Was this a turning point? In steroids!

I became a "**seminar junkie**". (But not taking **est,** given by Werner Erhard, who, after investigating, I determined to be pretty much a con man)

I was there when one of Alexander's instructor, Werner Erhard, announced he was forming est, Erhard Seminar Training). There were about 2000 people in the room at the Mark Hopkins Hotel, and here is an instructor announcing he is splitting off and forming his own awareness training.

In the lobby during a break, I asked Alexander "What do you think about this person right under your nose forming his own training outside of yours?" Alexander said "First there is the idea, then people start worshipping the person who has the idea, then they make images of the person who had the idea, then they build edifices to the person, then they create rituals around the person who had the idea, and then, people forget what the idea was."

Alexander was the most spiritual person that I ever met.

He made a turning point in my life, tipping me into spirituality and thinking outside the box. I am indebted to and happy about that insane night at the basement of Children's Hospital in San Francisco. When you become aware of normally unbelievable extra-ordinary events, it opens you up to the belief in other "unbelievable" possibilities (religion not necessary-Beyond Religion) that you normally wouldn't even consider.
Samuel Butler 7/7/2011

RELIGION INVOLVED IN THE VIOLENCE OF WORLD WAR II?

MUSSOLINI:
http://en.wikipedia.org/wiki/Benito_Mussolini His devout mother Rosa had him baptized into the Roman Catholic Church, and took her children to services every Sunday. Despite some other leanings, He wanted to persuade Catholics that "fascism was Catholic and he himself a believer who spent some of each day in prayer..." The Pope (PIUS XI) began referring to Mussolini as "a man sent by Providence."

HITLER:
From;
http://en.wikipedia.org/wiki/Adolf_Hitler's_religious_views
Hitler and Catholic ritual In his childhood, Hitler had admired the pomp of Catholic ritual and the hierarchical organization of the clergy. Later, he drew on these elements, organizing his party along hierarchical lines and including liturgical forms into events or using phraseology taken from hymns. Because of these liturgical elements, Hitler's Messiah-like status and the ideology's all-encompassing nature, the Nazi movement is sometimes termed a "political religion."

Hitler even used scripture (New Testament) as a rational against Jews: Also from the same above source: Hitler stated in a speech in 1927:

My feelings as a Christian points me to my Lord and Savior as a fighter. It points me to the man who once in loneliness, surrounded only by a few followers, recognized these Jews for what they were and summoned men to fight against them and who, God's truth! was greatest not as a sufferer but as a fighter. .. How terrific was His fight for the world against the Jewish poison.

Although he had other complex beliefs, according to Hitler's chief architect Albert Speer, Hitler remained a formal member of the Catholic Church until his death.

Stalin: At age 16, he was a seminary student, studying to become a priest in his native Georgia. He rebelled against the imperialist and religious order. Though he performed well there, he was expelled in 1899 after missing his final exams. The seminary's records suggest he was unable to pay his tuition fees. He became an atheist. (http://en.wikipedia.org/wiki/Joseph_Stalin)

Tojo (Hideki Tojo, Prime Minister of Japan from October 1941 to July 1944) The National State Religion of Japan (Ended by Douglas MacArthur in 1945) was Shintoism and it was the national state religion even in 0 AD. The Emperor was considered divine, a God, and no one could question his divinity. There also was Buddhist influences in Shinto.

From:
http://wiki.answers.com/Q/What_did_the_church_in_Japan_do_during_World_War_2

The entire history of Japan has been marked by internal warfare, assassination (e.g. one example is the Ninja) and harakiri (i.e. ritual suicide), revolution and swordsmanship. Few countries have had so violent a history, and much of this is still glorified in stage plays and movies featuring samurai knights and the cult of bushido ("the way of the warrior"). During bitter feuds between rival Buddhist sects, the streets of Kyoto, Japan's ancient capital, literally ran red with the blood of these priestly fighters and their henchmen.

A SHEAF OF LETTERS BLACKMAILING WOODROW WILSON AND 60 MILLION DEATHS

A story about unexpected consequences and how certain actions cause massive results-almost a butterfly effect in human not climatic terms.

A bunch of letters that Woodrow Wilson wrote to the wife of a Princeton professor that caused him to be blackmailed, that led to the U.S. being brought into WWI when it was stalemated and ready for peace to be made between the parties, which ended instead with onerous reparations to Germany, and the rise of Adolf Hitler, World War II and 60 million deaths, and now the Israeli - Palestinian Middle East conflicts today.

From Wikipedia, the free encyclopedia It was the Sussex, not the Lusitania...

The **Arabic pledge** was a promise made by the German Empire during World War I to limit unrestricted submarine warfare.

On May 7, 1915, Kaiserliche Marine U-boat U-20 sank the RMS Lusitania off the coast of Ireland. The Germans attacked the Lusitania without warning and the ship went down within 18 minutes. 1198 people on board died.[1] The passenger liner had departed from the port of New York City with many American citizens on board, 128 of whom were killed when the ship sank (including a member of the famous Vanderbilt family). The U.S. government condemned the German action and U.S. President Woodrow Wilson protested this violation of the United States' neutral rights and threatened to sever diplomatic relations with Germany.

In spite of this incident, Germany continued unrestricted submarine warfare until after the Arabic incident. On August 19, 1915, the British passenger liner Arabic was torpedoed by a

German U-boat. Approximately 40 passengers and crew were lost, including two Americans. Wilson again vigorously protested this attack. With the threat that the United States might join the war, the German government issued on September 18, 1915, what became known as the "Arabic pledge," which stated that Germany would warn non-military ships 30 minutes before they sank them to make sure the passengers and crew got out safely.

Germany broke this pledge on March 24, 1916, when a U-boat torpedoed the French ship Sussex. This led to the Sussex pledge.

Sussex pledge

From Wikipedia, the free encyclopedia

The **Sussex pledge** was a promise made in 1916 during World War I by Germany to the United States prior to the latter's entry into the war. Early in 1916, Germany had instituted a policy of unrestricted submarine warfare,[1] allowing armed merchant ships - but not passenger ships - to be torpedoed without warning. Despite this avowed restriction, a French cross-channel passenger ferry, the Sussex, was torpedoed without warning on March 24, 1916; the ship was severely damaged and about 50 lives were lost.[2] Although no U.S. citizens were killed in this attack, it prompted President Woodrow Wilson to declare that if Germany were to continue this practice, the United States would break diplomatic relations with Germany. Fearing the entry of the United States into World War I, Germany attempted to appease the United States by issuing, on May 4, 1916, the Sussex pledge, which promised a change in Germany's naval warfare policy. The primary elements of this undertaking were:

- Passenger ships would not be targeted;

- Merchant ships would not be sunk until the presence of weapons had been established, if necessary by a search of the ship;
- Merchant ships would not be sunk without provision for the safety of passengers and crew.

In 1917 Germany became convinced they could defeat the Allied Forces by instituting unrestricted submarine warfare before the United States could enter the war. The Sussex pledge was therefore rescinded in January 1917, thereby initiating the decisive stage of the so-called First Battle of the Atlantic. The resumption of unrestricted submarine warfare and the Zimmerman Telegram caused the United States to declare war on Germany on April 6, 1917.

If the Zionists support England and its Allies, James Malcolm Will Offer Them Palestine, and Then Important Zionists Will Get America into the War

From:
http://www.the7thfire.com/new_world_order/zionism/benja min_freedman/zionist_influence_on_congress.htm

He was passionately devoted to an Allied victory. While his home in London was being bombed by the Germans in 1944, he prepared the following account which speaks for itself. Mr. Malcolm feared he would not survive, and prepared the following which he deposited in the British Museum for the benefit of posterity. It has become one of the most important documents explaining how the United States was railroaded into World War I, and follows here:

"During one of my visits to the War Cabinet Office in Whitehall Gardens in the late summer of 1916 I found Sir Mark Sykes less buoyant than usual... I enquired what was troubling him... [H]e spoke of military deadlock in France, the growing menace of submarine warfare, the unsatisfactory situation which was developing in Russia and the general bleak outlook... [T]he Cabinet was looking anxiously for United States intervention...

"[H]e had thought of enlisting the substantial Jewish influence in the United States but had been unable to do so... [R]eports from America revealed a very pro-German tendency among the wealthy American-Jewish bankers and bond houses, nearly all of German origin, and among Jewish journalists who took their cue from them... I inquired what special argument or consideration had the Allies put forward to win over American Jewry... Sir Mark replied that he made use of the same argument as used elsewhere, viz., that we shall eventually win and it was better to be on the winning side...

"I informed him that there was a way to make American Jewry thoroughly pro-Ally, and make them conscious that only an Allied victory could be of permanent benefit to Jewry all over the world... I said to him, 'You are going the wrong way about it... do you know of the Zionist Movement?'... Sir Mark admitted ignorance of this movement and I told him something about it and concluded by saying, 'You can win the sympathy of the Jews everywhere in one way only, and that way is by offering to try and secure Palestine for them'... Sir Mark was taken aback. He confessed that what I had told him was something quite new and most impressive...

"He told me that Lord Milner was greatly interested to learn of the Jewish Nationalist movement but could not see any possibility of promising Palestine to the Jews... I replied that it seemed to me the only way to achieve the desired result, and mentioned that one of President Wilson's most intimate friends, for whose humanitarian views he has the greatest respect, was Justice Brandeis of the Supreme Court, who was a convinced Zionist...

"[I]f he could obtain from the War Cabinet an assurance that help would be given towards securing Palestine for the Jews, it was certain that Jews in all neutral countries would become pro-British and pro-Ally... I said I thought it would be sufficient if I were personally convinced of the sincerity of the Cabinet's intentions so that I could go to the Zionists and say, 'If you help the Allies, you will have the support of the British in securing Palestine for the Jews'...

"[A] day or two later, he informed me that the Cabinet had agreed to my suggestion and authorized me to open negotiations with the Zionists ... the messages which were sent to the Zionist leaders in Russia were intended to hearten them and obtain their support for the Allied cause... other messages were sent to Jewish leaders in neutral countries and the result was to strengthen the pro-Allied sympathies of Jews everywhere...

"[A] wealthy and influential anti-Zionist Jewish banker there was shown the telegram announcing the provisional promise of Palestine to the Jews... he was very much moved and said, 'How can a Jew refuse such a gift?'...

"[A]ll these steps were taken with the full knowledge and approval of Justice Brandeis, between whom and [Zionist leader] Dr. Weizmann there was an active interchange of cables... [A]fter many anxious weeks and months, my seed had borne fruit and the Government had become an ally of Zionism... the Declaration is dated 2nd November, 1917, and is known to history as the Balfour Declaration... its obligation to promise British help for the Jews to obtain Palestine."

Chaim Weizmann notified the leading Zionist in the USA, Supreme Court Justice Louis Dembitz Brandeis, that Great Britain had promised Palestine to "the Jews of the World" if President Wilson would declare war on Germany and come into the war as Great Britain's ally.

Supreme Court Justice Brandeis had been appointed to the United States Supreme Court at the suggestion of the powerful Jewish attorney Mr. Samuel Untermyer. Mr. Untermyer had been retained by a former sweetheart of then-President Woodrow Wilson to bring a breach-of-promise action against him shortly after he was installed in the White House. Mr. Untermyer's client was seeking forty thousand dollars from President Wilson which he was unable to raise. To be of assistance to his friend, President Wilson, in the predicament in which he found himself, Mr. Untermyer volunteered to pay the forty-thousand dollars to President Wilson's former sweetheart from his personal funds if in return President Wilson promised to appoint to the first vacancy on the United States Supreme Court the person Mr. Untermyer designated.

The day soon arrived when the vacancy on the Court occurred. Mr. Untermyer submitted the name of his friend, Louis Dembitz Brandeis, a [Jewish] Boston lawyer, to fill the vacancy. Mr. Untermyer explained that he was motivated by the fact that no Jew had ever occupied a seat on the United States Supreme Court, and for that reason he would like to see Mr. Brandeis appointed.

President Wilson and Justice Brandeis both knew the circumstances under which his appointment took place. They became close personal friends. President Wilson came to rely upon Justice Brandeis as an advisor in matters of state. When Chaim Weizmann confided in Justice Brandeis that he had made this arrangement with the British War Cabinet, he also told President Wilson that Germany had supplied provocation and justification for a US declaration of war against Germany. [But] President Wilson was running for re-election that year under the slogan "He Kept Us Out of War." Justice Brandeis was unable to urge President Wilson to declare war against Germany at that time. Further evidence of German "guilt" was needed. [And so, it was provided]

The publicity given to the alleged attack by Germany on the S.S. Sussex passenger ferry plying between Dover and Calais and the loss of 38 American lives led to the declaration of war by the USA against Germany on April 6, 1917. The S.S. Sussex had actually been concealed in a small port in the north of England and no American lives had been lost. The entrance of the USA into the war as Great Britain's ally in World War I resulted in the crushing defeat of Germany in 1918.

CONCLUSION

What would be wrong if you don't believe what I believe? Why can't we just get along? Does it hurt you if I believe differently?

Why is there hate, violence, and even war between what you believe and what I believe?

My answer is THAT is what the SCRIPTURES themselves COMMAND.

For example: Koran: Sura **9:5** But when the forbidden months are past, then fight and slay the Pagans (non-believers-like Christians and Jews-author) wherever ye find them, and seize them, beleaguer them, and lie in wait for them in every stratagem (of war);

Sura **9:123** O ye who believe! fight the unbelievers who gird you about, and let them find firmness in you: and know that Allah is with those who fear Him. If you believe in Allah, do not love anyone who is an un-believer, even if it is your father or brother;

God commanding Moses to kill:

"They fought against Midian, as **the LORD commanded Moses, and killed every man........Now kill all the boys [innocent kids]. And kill every woman who has slept with a man,** but save for yourselves every girl who has never slept with a man. (Numbers 31:7,17-18)"

Kill everything that "breathes" from humans and animals!

Deuteronomy 20:16 However, in the cities of the nations the Lord your God is giving you as an inheritance,

do not leave alive anything that breathes.

Talmud : This is the saying of Rabbi Simon ben Yohai: Tob shebe goyyim harog ("Even the best of the gentiles should all be killed").

Matthew: Jesus condemns entire cities to dreadful deaths and to the eternal torment of hell because they didn't care for his preaching. 11:20-24

Luke: Jesus says that entire cities will be violently destroyed and the inhabitants "thrust down to hell" for not "receiving" his disciples. 10:10-15

I say SHAME on those scriptures for all the hate, torture, and death directly encouraged and supported by those scriptures and the consequent actions by followers of those scriptures.

In the past, countless lives could have been saved if followers were more skeptical before being blind followers.

Then there are the sayings of the representatives of the religions. For Example:

Rabbi Yaacov Perrin said, "One million Arabs are not worth a Jewish fingernail." (NY Daily News, Feb. 28, 1994, p.6).

In wartime, it is OK to kill (innocent) women and children: (Rabbi) Shim'on Weiser in a letter to a Jewish Soldier.

I say SHAME on those who spread intolerance and hate because others don't believe the same as they do. (Islam, Christianity, and Judaism are good examples)

I say SHAME on the religions that sanction pedophilia, child molestation, and forcing marriages at shocking ages. (Islam and Judaism)

INTOLERANCE OF DIFFERENT BELIEFS

The Crusades: **WARS** fought over a period of nearly 200 years, between 1095 and 1291. Other campaigns in Spain and Eastern Europe continued into the 15th century.

The Inquisition (the Spanish Inquisition lasted from 1478-1834). Then the Holocaust.

Current history intolerance in the Middle East.

As you can see history has been propelled by religious beliefs resulted in a litany of Intolerance, Violence, Hate and War.

It's not just one religion. They are all involved. That is why I say "A SHAME on All Their Houses" and A SPELL (INCANTATION) for them to transform to **A MORE HUMANISTIC, LOVING AND PEACEFUL FUTURE.**

I say It is alright to be a skeptic on all of the religions.

Rather than focus on those who don't believe as you do, follow the Ten Principles for a Global Rational Humanism. (See the Code for Global Ethics on pages 5 and 90)

It will be a better world for it.

ABOUT THE AUTHOR

Samuel Butler is a graduate (B.A.) in Economics from University of California, Berkeley, 1959.

Former All-City Champion Pole Vaulter in San Francisco high schools

Former Captain United States Air Force (reserve) Navigator

Former President of the Toastmasters Club (Golden Gate Toastmasters) in San Francisco

Former Chief Appraiser of a Large Financial Institution in California

Former Vice President for Real Estate Acquisitions, United States Real Estate Corporation, Headquartered in the Bank of America Building in San Francisco

Owner, Founder, Butler Realty Group, focusing on Commercial Real Estate, located in the Transamerica Pyramid, San Francisco.

Successful Commercial Real Estate Broker (in Cushman and Wakefield, owned by Rockefeller) San Francisco

Now retired, plays golf, chess, and bridge. Founder, former President of Atlantis Energy, S.A., a biofuel corporation.

REFERENCES

1. http://www.biblewalks.com/Sites/TempleMount.html
See "Arab Period"

2. **"Religion Kills" is the title of Christopher Hitchens's Second Chapter in his book** *god is not Great, How Religion Poisons Everything* **.** Twelve Hachette Book Group USA, New York , 2007

3. Halakhah (in Judaism, all laws and ordinances evolved since biblical times to regulate worship and the daily lives of the Jewish people) purports to preserve and represent oral traditions stemming from the revelation on Mount Sinai or evolved on the basis of it. The legalistic nature of Halakhah also sets it apart from those parts of rabbinic, or Talmudic, literature that include history, fables, and ethical teachings (Haggadah). That Halakhah existed from ancient times is confirmed from nonpentateuchal passages of the Bible, where, for example, servitude is mentioned as a legitimate penalty for unpaid debts (2 Kings 4:1). Encyclopedia Britannica. In Yebamoth 60b, p. 404, Rabbi Zera disagrees that sex with girls under three years and one day should be endorsed as halakah.

4. http://individual.utoronto.ca/mfkolarcik/jesuit/herzog.html

5. http://www.biblebelievers.org.au/facts1.htm#Sanhedrin,%2055b-55a :
From the Talmud: Yebamoth 60b, p.402, 403 . A little girl under 3 years and a day, is eligible to live with a priest and marry him. And did.

Also: http://www.truthtellers.org/alerts/pedophiliasecret.html

6. http://www.biblebelievers.org.au/facts1.htm

7. http://www.truthtellers.org/alerts/pedophiliasecret.ht
ml

8. http://www.flw.ugent.be/cie/CIE2/shahak.htm

9. http://en.fairmormon.org/Moroni's_visit/Nephi_or
_Moroni

10. From We believe: doctrines and principles of the
Church of Jesus Christ of Latter Day... By Rulon T. Burton

http://books.google.com/books?id=KikT6wFDDBAC&pg=PA77
&lpg=PA77&dq=they+sprang.+He+also+said+that+the+fullness
+of+the+everlasting+gospel+was+contained+in+it&source=bl&
ots=1UqJps2kG4&sig=PPfUzsbgCZcHAq5LcYJDRML-
a80&hl=en&ei=5vgLTLjWDoH58AaPyryOBw&sa=X&oi=book_re
sult&ct=result&resnum=2&ved=0CBcQ6AEwAQ#v=onepage&q
&f=false

11. http://www.wcc-
coe.org/wcc/what/interreligious/cd39-03.html

12. http://www.facebook.com/group.php?gid=3927310070
4

13. http://dissidentvoice.org/Articles9/Parenti_Tibet.htm

14. http://www.michaelparenti.org/**Tibet**

15. http://hi.baidu.com/lovesue/blog/item/207722a4be41
d5f39052eec1.html

16. http://www.studentsforafreetibet.org/article.php?id=4
24

INDEX

D

E

F

forgeries · 3, 13, 14, 15, 40
Fortune · 89
France · 50, 127
Frederic Farrar · 10

G

Gallilee · 14
Gautama Siddhartha · 104
Gaza · 54
Genocide · 60, 68
Gentiles · 70, 72, 73
George Washington · 7, 18
Georgia · 124
Gerd-R. Puin
   Dr. · 92
German · 125, 126, 128, 130
Germany · 13, 125, 126, 127, 129,
   130, 131
Gibeah · 54
Gnosticism · 43
God · 5, 1, 3, 8, 15, 18, 22, 32, 33, 45,
   46, 48, 49, 52, 53, 54, 55, 56, 58,
   60, 64, 65, 66, 68, 73, 77, 89, 97,
   99, 109, 112, 113, 123, 124, 132
goddess · 8, 36
Goddess · 88, 89, 90, 91
gold plates · 8, 96, 97, 100
Goldstein's · 73
Gordon Stein · 13
Gospel · 12, 27, 40
Greek · 5, 16, 61

H

Hagarene · 92
Halakhah · 71, 136
Ham · 56
Hamas · 86
harakiri · 124
heathen · 6, 9, 47, 48, 78
Hebrew · 60, 67, 68, 73
hell · 35, 36, 59, 133
Hesus · 7
Hilton Hotema · 43
Historia Ecclesiastica · 9
Hitchens · 1, 3, 136

Hitler · 9, 123, 124, 125
Hittites · 53
Hivites · 53
homosexuality · 64, 65
Horus · 6

I

Ibn Kathir · 83
Ilham Mahdi al Assi · 84
imbalance · 39, 111
India · 6, 91, 117, 118
Inquisition · 1, 39, 41, 134
intolerance · 3, 1, 39, 133, 134
Intolerance · 1, 9, 33, 134
Ireland · 26, 50, 125
Irenaeus · 14
Ishtar · 36
Islam · 3, 8, 82, 83, 86, 88, 89, 90, 92,
   111, 133
Israel · 54, 62, 68, 75, 79
Israelis · 68

J

J. V. Chelvanayakam · 108
Jabeshgilead · 56
Jack Miles · 113
Jacob Burckhardt · 7
James Madison · 6, 7, 17, 18
JAMES MADISON · 21
Japan · 124
Jebusites · 53
Jerry Falwell · 18
Jesus · 7, 10, 11, 12, 13, 14, 16, 17,
   18, 19, 20, 27, 35, 36, 38, 39, 40,
   42, 43, 45, 46, 52, 57, 59, 92, 96,
   102, 103, 104, 133, 137
Jesus Christ · 40
Jewish · 8, 5, 16, 28, 29, 33, 61, 62,
   67, 68, 69, 71, 72, 73, 74, 75, 76,
   88, 111, 124, 128, 129, 130, 133,
   136
Jews · 19, 61, 62, 67, 68, 71, 73, 75,
   76, 81, 82, 83, 123, 128, 129, 132
John · 7, 16, 18, 27, 32, 33, 42, 46,
   57, 95, 98, 121

R

Rabbi Simon ben Yohai · 133
Rafea A. · 111
Rajagraha · 104
religion · 3, 5, 6, 7, 8, 1, 3, 4, 5, 6, 8,
    11, 15, 16, 18, 21, 22, 24, 29, 30,
    36, 38, 39, 40, 52, 92, 93, 105,
    109, 112, 121, 123, 124, 134
religions · 3, 1, 3, 6, 13, 16, 30, 33,
    42, 61, 88, 105, 133, 134
Religious · 1, 3, 16, 17, 91
Republican · 93
Richard Bock · 117
Richard Sipe · 50
Rick Perry · 18
Rick Santorum · 18
Rights · 22, 78, 84
Robert M. Price
    Dr. · 92
Roberto Calvi · 32
Roman · 5, 6, 7, 8, 13, 16, 37, 42, 50,
    123
Rome · 6, 13, 31, 36, 42

S

Sabbath · 52, 65
Sai Baba · 117, 118
Saladin · 73
Samaritan · 55
Samuel Untermyer · 130
San Francisco · 28, 29, 102, 118, 119,
    120, 121, 135
San Leandro · 28
San'a · 83
Sanhedrin · 70, 75, 76, 77, 78, 79,
    136
Santa Clara · 28
Sapphira · 57
Sargon
    the Great · 61
Satan's · 75
Savior · 8, 15, 97, 123
Schipper, J.E. · 111
scripture · 1, 91, 123
scriptures · 3, 73, 91, 133

Seattle · 31
Senator · 13
Serapeum · 7, 9
Sharia Law · 86
Sharon G. · 111
Shia's · 39
Shiites · 1
Shinto · 124
Shirley Maclaine · 117
Simeon · 54, 75, 76, 77, 79
Simon ben Yohai · 68
Sinaiticus · 10, 27
Socrates · 9
Solomon · 62
Soncino · 76
Spanish Inquisition · 134
spirit · 7, 53, 110
spiritual · 26, 75, 117, 121
Śrī Lankā · 107
St Paul · 45
St. Catherine's Monastery · 27
St. Paul's cathedral · 36
Stalin · 124
Stone · 89, 113
Sun · 33, 41, 86, 89, 90
Sunnis · 1
superstitions · 9, 110
Sussex · 125, 126, 127, 131
Switzerland · 119
Systemic Theology · 26

T

Tacitus · 13
Tafsir · 83
Taliban · 111
Talmud · 67, 68, 70, 72, 73, 74, 75,
    76, 77, 78, 79, 80, 133, 136
Tamil Eelam
    Liberation Tigers of · 107
Tanakh · 62, 67
Tel Aviv · 62
Telfer · 1, 93, 94
temples · 5, 9, 65, 112
TESTAMENT · 7, 58, 60
    WOMEN IN THE NEW · 58
Testimonies · 8
Testimonium Flavianum · 13